QUANTITATIVE INVESTING

STRATEGIES TO EXPLOIT STOCK MARKET ANOMALIES FOR ALL INVESTORS

FRED PIARD

HARRIMAN HOUSE LTD

3A Penns Road
Petersfield
Hampshire
GU32 2EW
GREAT BRITAIN

Tel: +44 (0)1730 233870
Email: enquiries@harriman-house.com
Website: www.harriman-house.com

First published in Great Britain in 2013

ISBN: 9780857193001

British Library Cataloguing in Publication Data
A CIP catalogue record for this book can be obtained from the British Library.

CONTENTS

DISCLAIMER

THE INFORMATION PROVIDED IN THIS BOOK is for educational purposes only. It is not investment advice. Before deciding to invest in financial markets you should carefully consider your investment objectives, level of experience, and risk appetite. The possibility exists that you could sustain a loss of some or all of your initial investment. You should seek advice from an independent financial advisor if you have any doubt.

All products, ETFs, tools and websites quoted in this book are the property and trademarks of their respective issuers. This work provides information about various investment methods. It does not constitute an offer, a financial promotion, or a solicitation to purchase or sell any financial instruments.

No representation is being made that any investor will achieve results similar to those discussed here. The past performance of a system or methodology is not necessarily indicative for the future. The results presented in this book are mostly based on simulations. They have been made as realistic as possible. However there is a risk of errors from the data, software, and human operator.

CFTC RULE 4.41 – HYPOTHETICAL OR SIMULATED PERFORMANCE RESULTS HAVE CERTAIN LIMITATIONS. UNLIKE AN ACTUAL PERFORMANCE RECORD, SIMULATED RESULTS DO NOT REPRESENT ACTUAL TRADING. ALSO, SINCE THE TRADES HAVE NOT BEEN EXECUTED, THE RESULTS MAY HAVE UNDER-OR-OVER COMPENSATED FOR THE IMPACT, IF ANY, OF CERTAIN MARKET FACTORS, SUCH AS LACK OF LIQUIDITY. SIMULATED TRADING PROGRAMS IN GENERAL ARE ALSO SUBJECT TO THE FACT THAT THEY ARE DESIGNED WITH THE BENEFIT OF HINDSIGHT. NO REPRESENTATION IS BEING MADE THAT ANY ACCOUNT WILL OR IS LIKELY TO ACHIEVE PROFIT OR LOSSES SIMILAR TO THOSE SHOWN.

eBook edition

As a buyer of the print edition of *Quantitative Investing* you can now download the eBook edition free of charge to read on an eBook reader, your smartphone or your computer. Simply go to:

http://ebooks.harriman-house.com/QI

or point your smartphone at the QRC below.

You can then register and download your free eBook.

Follow us on Twitter – **@harrimanhouse** – for the latest on new titles and special offers.

www.harriman-house.com

 Harriman House

ABOUT THE AUTHOR

FRED PIARD GAINED EXTENSIVE EXPERIENCE in the software industry, information systems consulting and marketing before discovering an interest in the financial markets. Self-taught in this field, he puts into practice what he learnt from his previous activities to build his own methodology. From his years in research he has the ability to combine a systemic point of view and an analytic approach. As a software architect he knows that the things that work the best in the long term are the simplest. As a consultant he experienced the real economy through various sectors: energy, banking, healthcare, manufacturing and public administration. And he learned from marketing that human group behavior can sometimes be modeled, but never predicted. He has a PhD in computer science, an MSc in software engineering and an MSc in civil engineering.

PREFACE

Who this book is for

THIS BOOK WAS WRITTEN FOR ANYONE looking for simple, effective and low-risk investing strategies. The strategies described in the following pages can be managed in just five minutes a week, sometimes much less, making them suitable for investors with a full-time job. Although this is not a book for short term traders, they may discover here that, in the era of high frequency trading, a classical approach to the market may be more profitable than expected.

The book is designed to be short and actionable. It is also relatively simple; nevertheless the idea of simplicity is not the same for everyone. In case a word or concept is not clear, the reader may like to refer to an online knowledge base such as Wikipedia or Investopedia. It may help to have some knowledge of statistics to understand the more technical parts of the book. However, the understanding and implementation of the strategies needs only a logical mind and to feel comfortable with browsing online financial data sources. No specific background in finance or mathematics is needed.

All strategies can be implemented without purchasing any additional product or service. However, the appendix presents an offer for the tool that has been used for the studies in this book, it just makes the implementation simpler and faster.

What the book covers

All the strategies presented in this book share some common characteristics:

- They are **inspired by academic and professional publications**. Their presentation, simulation, interpretation, combination and choice of instruments may be original in this book, but the concepts have been known and documented for years, some of them for decades. This is an indication of their robustness.

- They use **only stocks and non-leveraged Exchange-Traded Funds** (ETFs) available in the U.S. stock market. The concepts may well work with other instruments and in other markets, but no representation is made about the expected results.

- All the instruments used are **very liquid**. However the use of orders with a limit price is recommended.

- All the strategies are **long only**. There is no short selling.

Structure of the book

The core content has been organized in chapters based on a strategy classification. It is preceded by a discussion of methodology, and followed by some tips and warnings for readers developing their own strategies. After the conclusion, the appendix provides an extract of research for a new kind of indicator.

ACKNOWLEDGEMENTS

SPECIAL THANKS to Stephen Eckett at Harriman House, for his help from the initial idea to the final manuscript.

INTRODUCTION

THERE ARE TWO WAYS TO LEARN INVESTING: the hard way and the smart way. Most people start with the hard way – as I did.

When I decided to manage my own money, I started by following the financial media; I bought shares in a company and a tracker with a lot of confidence and then forgot them for three years. I also forgot this quote by Woody Allen:

> "Confidence is what you have before you understand the problem."

That was my first active experience in the financial market. I was lucky enough that my profits just about offset my losses – but I was aware that it was just luck. So I decided to follow the People Who Know. I tried half a dozen paid services. The result of my follow-the-gurus period was no better than when I started. However I had begun to learn something about the market.

The next stage was to study some technical indicators and patterns, and have a go at day-trading. I proved to myself that it could work, but with a lot of stress and time and it conflicted with my lifestyle. I like the idea of putting money to work for one's life, not the opposite.

I found a better way for me when I began to scan with screeners and simulation tools the history of fundamental and technical data on thousands of stocks and ETFs. I enjoyed this intellectual playing field: exploring dozens of strategies, coding hundreds of variations, performing thousands of simulations.

With a set of reasonably good strategies, quantitative investing allows one to act in the market at specific pre-planned times. It is possible to work on this just once a week or month, and ignore charts and the news. It removes most of the doubts and emotions with the discipline of keeping a long-term vision and sensible money management. And it can be a complement or a replacement to legacy investing strategies.

This approach suited me.

A scientific approach to investing

Scientific investment strategies have been pursued for decades, not only by hedge funds but also by more traditional managers. All types of data may be used, provided that they can be measured: fundamental data, technical indicators, market sentiment, and newsfeeds. The assets managed by quantitative funds have grown first slowly, then in an explosive way to an estimated 1.5 trillion dollars before the 2008 crisis. Victims of overcrowding and excessive leveraging, they fell to a quarter of the previous value in 2009.

But what exactly is quantitative investing?

Although it has been mainly developed and used by technologically advanced funds, it cannot be defined by actors or technology. It is a scientific approach based on hypotheses and empirical testing. It is not limited to only sophisticated funds – some techniques are accessible to individual investors.

There are various possible definitions of quantitative investing. This is mine:

Identifying reasonable and measurable hypotheses about behaviours of the financial market so as to make investment decisions with an acceptable confidence in expected returns and risks.

The main advantages in using quantitative models are:

- making the investment process independent of opinions and emotions (the most important factor for an individual investor), and

- making it reproducible by anyone at anytime (the most important factor for a fund)

The first risk comes from misinterpretations of what is a "reasonable hypothesis" and an "acceptable confidence" in the definition. In other words, choosing a bad strategy because of wrong or incomplete criteria.

Another risk is that an idea that has been good in the past may become bad in the future. On the one hand, some techniques are condemned to a shorter and shorter lifespan due to accelerated information diffusion. On the other hand, some old ideas have continued to perform quite well in recent years. My aim here is to shed new light on the second category.

CHAPTER 1:

METHODOLOGY

THIS CHAPTER FIRST DEFINES the market anomalies that will be used in the strategies and then the criteria to evaluate them. It also lists the tools and requirements to execute strategies. Finally, it ends with a brief overview of the hypotheses, vocabulary and formalisms used in the book.

FOCUS ON SIMPLE BASIC PRINCIPLES

This book is built around four concepts. Four categories of anomalies that have been used for decades by successful investors to beat the market. Four concepts that have continued to beat the market in recent years, despite the fact that they are well-recognised.

The four aces of our game are:

1. market timing,
2. momentum,
3. seasonals,
4. valuation.

Before looking at these in some detail, let's be clear: there's nothing magic here – these anomalies don't work every time.

They are also controversial; you will find articles claiming that they don't work. These articles are generally poorly documented and written or sponsored by people that have an interest in making individual investors believe that they don't work. On the other hand, you can find very well documented academic articles claiming that they have brought a significant statistical advantage to those who were able to apply them with consistency for decades.

Will these anomalies continue to work?

Nobody can be sure, however studying the past over a long period is the best way to plan the future. Please note that I have used the word *plan*, not *predict*.

We will now look at these four categories of anomalies in the market.

1. Market timing

The idea of market timing is to get out of an asset class when an indicator or a combination of indicators enters a risky zone. Market timing is generally built on technical indicators, typically moving averages.

A *moving average* is an average price on a trailing period of N time units. The values to average are the prices on close of each time unit (often day). We will see examples and applications of moving averages in the next chapter.

Sophisticated aggregate indicators may also be used. Some examples:

- put/call ratio for options on an index derivative or a set of stocks,
- investor sentiment surveys,
- number of S&P 100 stocks above their 200-day moving average,
- ratio of bullish/bearish chart patterns in a set of stocks,
- average provisional EPS for S&P 500 companies.

Using an appropriate indicator, market timing generally works quite well with global indexes.

2. Momentum

Momentum is generally defined as the return (relative increase in price) between two points in time separated by a fixed interval:

(P2-P1)/P1

or as the ratio between the prices at these two points:

P2/P1

When used as a relative strength indicator to rank two or more assets, both definitions are equivalent. Momentum is an indicator of the average speed of price on a timescale defined by the interval. The most used intervals by investors are 1, 3, 6 and 12 months, or their equivalent in trading days.

Investing on momentum is investing on the current trend. The idea is that the price has a kind of inertia and is likely to continue in the same direction if its speed is high enough.

Momentum generally works well with global and specialized indexes (sectors for example).

3. Seasonals

Many human activities have seasonal cycles. Seasonal patterns can be identified in any financial market: indexes, individual stocks, currencies, commodities, etc.

The stock market's seasonal cycle is not reliable every year, but it is powerful over the long term. Seasonal patterns on the Dow Jones have been documented since the 1920s, but scientific explanations for their consistency and resistance to arbitrage have failed in spite of interesting academic publications.

You have probably already heard of some of the best-known effects:

- *Sell in May and Go Away*: the stock market tends to be relatively weak for a few months from May

- *Halloween Effect*: the odds are favorable again in November and a rally may take place before Halloween.

- *Santa Claus Rally*: December is usually a good month for stocks.

The terms "Sell in May…" and "Halloween" effects are often used to name the same annual cycle. In fact, they are separate effects with different (and still unclear) theoretical explanations, giving together an annual cycle.

Seasonal patterns are more reliable for diversified indexes. It is more complicated for sectors because of the superposition of different cycles.

4. Valuation

Calculating a company's value and identifying possible anomalies in the stock price is the field of fundamental analysis. Three main factors influence the perception of the value on the market:

1. **Intrinsic Value**. It relies on a snapshot of the latest accounting data of the company (generally last quarter's earnings).

2. **Growth History**. Analysts use different metrics to measure growth. The stock price has more resilience if the company has a steady growth record; but investors may also overreact to an acceleration or deceleration in growth.

3. **Dividend History**. A steady dividend yield and, even better, a steadily increasing dividend yield, is an attracting thing for buy-and-hold investors.

Note: in elaborating valuation strategies I care less about what is the "real value" of a stock, than on identifying combinations of fundamental data that have a significant probability to move the price.

EVALUATING STRATEGIES

This sub-chapter covers mathematical formulas and concepts. They help you to understand the ratios used to evaluate strategies, but they are not necessary to implement them. You may want to skip this section, or read it again later, if you find it complicated.

Average return

The average return of an investment can be calculated on any time unit, from days to years. Moreover, there are different mathematical ways of "averaging" a data series. Unless otherwise stated, *average return* in this book means the Compound Annual Growth Rate (CAGR).

If the total return of a period of Q years is T%, the CAGR is:

CAGR = (1+(T/100))$^{1/Q}$ -1

In words, it is the hypothetical constant annual return that would have given the total return, reinvesting gains. Therefore, it is a compound return.

For example, let's suppose that a strategy has a 50% total return over 2 years.

It's CAGR is 0.225 = 22.5%.

If a strategy multiplied capital by 10 in 10 years (+900%), the CAGR is 25.9%.

The number of years does not need to be an integer; the CAGR may be calculated on 10 years as well as on only 6 months. Of course, a CAGR calculated for a short period has little significance regarding a strategy's performance.

An average return on a long period is an imprecise indicator. When evaluating in detail a strategy, I take the time to calculate the CAGR for each year during the evaluation period. The CAGR variations helps to understand the behavior in different market conditions.

Drawdown

The drawdown is sometimes defined as "the decline in value from a peak to a bottom". However things are not so simple: *which peak* and *which bottom*?

First I will define the drawdown at the present time, then in the past, then define the maximum drawdown, which is really the concept of interest. Doing so I hope to explain in simple words that the maximum drawdown is the result of what scientists call a *recursive calculation*.

The current value of drawdown is usually defined as the loss in percentage terms between the highest portfolio value and the current portfolio value. For example, if the highest value was 500,000 and the current value is 450,000, the drawdown is:

(50-45)/50 = 0.1 = 10%

By definition, if the current value is at its highest point, the drawdown is zero.

The drawdown at a date in the past is the loss in percentage between the highest value before or at this date, and the value at this date.

The maximum drawdown for a period of time is the maximum of the drawdowns for all dates in the period.

If we define the drawdown at a time t as a mathematical function DD(t) and the maximum drawdown as another function DDM(t), then:

DDM(t) = max (DDM(t-1), DD(t))

Here comes recursivity: DDM at time t is defined from its own value in the previous state at t-1. In finance, time is discrete: the variable t is an integer. It may measure any time unit in your charting tool, from tick to year.

That was about the drawdown depth. Another important aspect of drawdown is its length (or duration).

The maximum drawdown duration on a period of time is the longest interval (in days, weeks, months) during which the portfolio (or strategy) has not made a new high. The longest drawdown is not always the deepest.

In this book drawdowns are generally calculated using the daily close price. The intraday drawdowns may be deeper. For leveraged and very volatile trading strategies, it is better to use intraday lows and highs.

Be careful when reading studies, sometimes drawdowns are calculated using weekly or monthly close prices, which may be quite inaccurate to represent what really happens to a portfolio.

There are various drawdown-based formulas to evaluate the strength and robustness of an investment. The simplest is the Sterling ratio:

Average Annual Return/(Maximum Drawdown + 10%)

The higher the ratio, the better.

Sharpe ratio

The Sharpe ratio is a risk-adjusted performance indicator: the higher, the better. It takes into account the difference of the average return with a benchmark, and its volatility. The Sharpe ratio promotes strategies that have good *and* steady returns.

The formula is:

(<R>-Ro)/Std

<R> is the expected return, usually the average annual return is used.

Ro is a benchmark return, usually a risk-free rate or a global index return (e.g. S&P 500).

Std is the standard deviation. In the original definition of 1966 it was the standard deviation of the return. Since a revision in 1994 the standard deviation of the excess return (return minus Ro) is preferred.

I doubt that you will ever have to calculate a Sharpe ratio yourself, nowadays software does this. If you don't have such software, look for *free sharpe ratio spreadsheet* and *free sharpe ratio calculator* in an internet search engine.

Sortino ratio

The drawback of the Sharpe ratio is that it penalizes strategies that have sometimes exceptionally good years (because they have a higher volatility). The Sortino ratio corrects that, taking into account only the "negative" volatility.

The formula is:

(<R>-Ro)/Stdn

<R> and Ro have the same definitions as for the Sharpe ratio.

Stdn is the standard deviation calculated only on negative returns. A variant is to calculate it on negative excess returns (returns minus Ro).

Kelly Criterion

Both previous ratios rely on Gaussian statistical hypotheses. It means that the data series are supposed to be attracted to average values by a kind of gravity whose strength is in inverse relation with the standard deviation. The reality is more chaotic.

Gambling theory is supposed to be more general. The Kelly criterion is the best known ratio in this field. Its value gives the theoretical percentage of an available capital to bet on a strategy to maximize performance in the long term. In reality this should be considered as the maximum limit. I use it as a probabilistic indicator of robustness. The higher the result, the more reliable the strategy.

Nevertheless the Kelly criterion also relies on probabilistic hypotheses: the probability of gain and the average gain/average loss ratio are supposed to be constant.

There is no unique and perfect ratio to assess the quality of a strategy. It's better to use several.

The formula is:

K = P- (1-P)/W

where:

W is the average win/average loss ratio.

P is the probability to win. The experimental probability of the data sample is generally used (number of positive returns divided by total number of returns).

As a game theory indicator it is designed to be calculated not on annual returns but on the whole set of trades or points of decision. It makes sense when the set of data is big enough.

The Kelly criterion is invariant with leveraging. Therefore it can be used as a robustness indicator, but not as a risk indicator.

The following technical note is for readers with a scientific background.

TECHNICAL NOTE

It is possible to take into account that P and W are not so constant or quite different from the experimental values. A simple differential calculus on K gives:

$dK/dP = 1+1/W$

$dK/dW = (1-P)/W^2$

In the following strategies W is between 0.9 and 1.7 and P is between 0.5 and 0.7:

So

$dK/dP > 1.59$

and

$dK/dW < 0.62$

It means that the Kelly criterion is at least 2.5 times more sensitive to a variation in P than to a variation in W. So the incertitude on W may reasonably be ignored.

When I want to take into account the incertitude on P, I replace the experimental probability with the statistical probability for a 95% confidence interval. This is a value (let's name it P95) such that the real probability to win has a 95% odds to be better than P95. The Kelly criterion using P95 (let's name it K95) adds a security margin, especially when the data sample is not big enough. You can find how to calculate a probability with a confidence interval in a book on statistics.

Limits

Strategies can be evaluated and compared if they can be simulated on a period long enough with a set of sufficient decision points (or trades), covering various market conditions. The longer the period, the better the evaluation.

However, even with statistics on data over decades, take the figures with caution. A high numercial precision makes no sense, and a difference of 2% in average return between two strategies may be random.

Interpreting the criteria?

Now that I have defined the evaluation criteria for investing strategies, you would probably like the acceptable values for these criteria. Unfortunately, there is no definitive answer. In fact these criteria should be taken as relative values to compare investment strategies. No absolute conclusion should be made about them.

Their interpretation depends on the:

- **market conditions** during the period of evaluation,
- **trading rhythm**, the expected average return and risk-adjusted ratios are not the same for a day-trader and an investor rebalancing his portfolio once a year,
- **capital**, a fund with $10 billion of assets under management doesn't have the same constraints as an individual investing $10,000,
- **objective, risk profile, leverage**, etc...

For example, an individual investor may be happy with a Sharpe ratio of 0.8. Whereas a Sharpe ratio above 2 might be required by a professional day-trader.

I can tell you some criteria to select the weekly and monthly strategies I use for my newsletters and my own account (these strategies are not described in this book):

- the criteria are calculated on **10-year simulations** or more,
- **minimum CAGR**: 15%,
- **maximum drawdown**: 30% and lower than (or reasonably close to) the CAGR,
- **minimum Sortino ratio**: 0.9,
- as for **Kelly's criterion**, when I calculate it I generally reject strategies with values below 0.2 (20%).

These are the criteria for *individual* strategies. I think that it is wise to combine at least three strategies with different rationales, and try to get a global CAGR above 20% and a global maximum drawdown below 15%.

These criteria give an edge, not a guarantee. Past performance, simulated *or real*, is never a guarantee for the future.

THE COST OF A DRAWDOWN

Increasingly, investors are using simulations on the past (or *backtests*) to make investment decisions for the future. Unfortunately they often make two mistakes: they assume that a simulation has a predictive power and they focus on the return. Whereas the main interest of a simulation is in evaluating the risk of a strategy. It can be assessed on two levels:

- The **robustness** of the game. Sterling ratio, Sortino ratio and Kelly criterion are good indicators for this purpose: the higher, the better. Looking at the three gives a better picture of a strategy.

- The **history of drawdowns**. The most obvious indicators are the maximum drawdown (maximum relative loss in %) and the maximum drawdown length (maximum duration in loss): the lower, the better.

Two other significant data may be calculated from the drawdown:

THE GAIN NECESSARY TO MAKE UP FOR A LOSS

If the drawdown is x, the formula is:

$f(x) = x/(1-x)$

For example:

When a portfolio has a 30% drawdown, it needs a 43% gain to recover:

$0.30/(1-0.30) = 0.428$

When it has a 50% drawdown, it needs a 100% gain:

$0.5/0.5 = 1$

This is an indication of the *drawdown cost*, or the effort to recover.

THE ADDITIONAL GAIN NECESSARY TO MAKE UP FOR AN ADDITIONAL 1% IN DRAWDOWN

The formula is:

$$df(x)/dx = 1/(1-x)^2$$

For example:

When a portfolio has a 30% drawdown and falls to a 31% drawdown, it needs an additional 2% gain to restore the initial state (zero drawdown):

$$1/(1-0.30)^2 = 2.04$$

When an additional 1% occurs at a 50% drawdown, it needs a 4% additional gain to restore the initial state:

$$1/(1-0.50)^2 = 4$$

It is a kind of *drawdown marginal cost*.

TOOLS AND REQUIREMENTS

DATA SOURCES

For any stock or ETF ticker symbol listed in this book, you can find more information on financial websites. For example in Yahoo! Finance: you go to the home page and enter the ticker in the *Enter Symbol* field, then click the *Get Quotes* button. Once on the result page, tabs on the left allow you to see corporate information, news, technical and fundamental data.

For strategies with ETFs, you need to compare ETF prices and moving averages. There are various free online charting platforms like Yahoo! Finance, Google Finance, Stockcharts.com, Freestockcharts.com. I prefer the latter for its design and versatility.

For strategies involving stocks, you need a screener on fundamental data. At the time of writing, the best free screener I know is on Finviz.com.

Fundamental data may differ from one data supplier to another. As simulations are impossible on Finviz, there is no way to compare backtest results. Finviz is considered as a reliable source of information, but if you think you have better tools, feel free to use them.

SIMULATION SOFTWARE

You don't need simulation software to implement the strategies described in this book. However I think it is necessary to tell you which tool I have used and why.

When I was looking for a simulation tool to test strategies, the requirements were:

- covering the widest possible set of ETFs and stocks on the U.S. market,

- reliable end-of-day data feed (the aim is not day-trading),

- historical data for 10 years or more,

- technical and fundamental screening,

- keeping dead companies in simulations (no survivor bias),

- time-stamped fundamental data (no look-ahead bias),

- realistic simulation parameters (slippage/commission),

- independent software editor or platform,

- affordable for an individual investor.

I eventually chose Portfolio123.

All simulation charts in this book are courtesy of Portfolio123. This tool is not necessary to execute the strategies, but it does allow the strict duplication of them. [The appendix explains how to obtain an extended free trial and the code of some strategies (this offer may be limited in time).]

To calculate maximum drawdowns and lengths, flat returns (return with a fixed amount invested, without compounding), probabilities with a confidence interval and Kelly formula, I use spreadsheets in LibreOffice Calc (a free equivalent of Microsoft Excel®).

COMMON HYPOTHESES, VOCABULARY AND PRESENTATION

Unless otherwise stated, all the strategies and simulations in this book share the following characteristics:

- orders are simulated on open price,

- the data used for calculations and decisions are the data available after the close of the market the day before,

- gains and dividends are reinvested.

I call *rebalancing* the double action of:

- making a decision to change (or not) the assets in a portfolio,

- changing the position sizes in a portfolio (for example to keep an equal weight).

In this book, I will mainly describe strategies where portfolios are rebalanced every week (*weekly rebalancing*) or every 4 weeks (*4-week rebalancing*). The expression *monthly rebalancing,* sometimes used in this book, designates a 4-week rebalancing.

Each rebalancing date is a *decision point*.

All dates use the US system (i.e. mm/dd/yyyy).

The word *day* is used for trading day. There are usually 5 trading days in a week.

Strategy definition

Strategies are described with the following table format:

Name	Designation to identify the strategy later in the book
Assets	List of the ticker symbols that may be part of the portfolio
Simulation period	Time interval on which the backtest is run. Defined by a *starting date* and an *end date*.
Re-balanced	Weekly or 4-week
Positions	Number of positions in portfolio. Each *position* is defined by a ticker symbol and an amount of money (or % of portfolio).
Maximum size	Maximum size of an individual position in % of the portfolio value
Rules	List of conditions checked at each rebalancing date for assets to be bought or kept. The assets in portfolio that don't comply any more are sold.
Leverage	1 (no leverage) or 2 (leveraged twice)
Transactions costs	% of the transaction modelling the spread and brokerage commission
Benchmark	Reference to a standard investment, usually the S&P 500 Index or its ETF SPY (which includes dividends)

The *inception date* of an ETF is the first day the product was available for trading.

For an ETF strategy, the starting date cannot precede any of the assets' inception dates.

The result of a simulation will be summarized by statistical data and a chart representing the portfolio total return (%) in time.

The charts will also sometimes track the number of positions in portfolio (*#Pos*) and the percentage of positions changing on each rebalancing date (*turnover*).

CHAPTER SUMMARY

- This book explains investment strategies that are simple enough to be executed in a few minutes per week or per month by an individual investor.

- It is focused on stocks and ETFs. Strategies are classified in four categories: market timing, momentum, seasonal patterns, valuation.

- The criteria to evaluate strategies include: average return, drawdown depth, drawdown duration, Sharpe ratio, Sortino ratio, Sterling ratio, Kelly criterion.

- The tools, vocabulary, hypotheses and generic presentation of a strategy are defined in this chapter.

The four following chapters focus on the four categories of anomalies previously explained.

Let's begin with market timing.

CHAPTER 2:

MARKET TIMING

THE WORD *MARKET* DESIGNATES the systems, structures, institutions and procedures that allow buyers and sellers to exchange liquid assets. It may apply at different levels from a class of assets (stocks, bonds, commodities, currencies) or a class of instruments (futures, options) to an individual asset (particular stock, metal, currency pair, etc...). A *bull market* is a market where prices are trending up, a *bear market* is a market where they are trending down. *Market timing* is the science or art to detect with a reasonable probability when a market is turning from *bullish* to *bearish,* or the reverse.

This chapter explores various strategies based on simple timing rules, applying them to diversified stock indexes, then to sectors, and finally to global asset classes.

S&P 500 MARKET TIMING

The best known market timing indicators use simple moving averages.

The simple moving average (SMA) on N periods is the arithmetic average of the closing prices for the N latest periods. It is calculated at the close of a period p:

SMA20(p) = (close(p) + close(p-1) +....+ close(p-N+1))/N

The most popular moving averages in market timing are on 20, 50 and 200 periods on a daily time scale. The idea is to consider that the market is bullish when the price is above a particular SMA, and bearish when it is below it. A variant is to consider that the market is bullish when a short SMA is above a long SMA and bearish when it is the contrary.

Here is an example, with SMA50 and SMA200 on the S&P 500 index chart from 2004 to 2013:

Chart 2.1: example chart with moving averages

Chart courtesy of Freestockcharts.com

In fact the chart above shows weekly SMAs. When using weekly charts, the 200-day SMA is close to the 40-week SMA and the 50-day SMA is close to the 10-week SMA. Graphically you cannot see the difference. Nevertheless they are not equal. The moving averages are calculated on daily close in one case, on weekly close in the other case. The next calculations and simulations will be executed with the true daily SMAs.

EXAMPLE STRATEGIES

We are looking for strategies on ETFs, so let's see what happens if:

1. we are invested in SPY (SPDR S&P 500 ETF Trust) when the price is above the red line (SMA200) and otherwise out of the market.

2. we are invested in SPY when the blue line (SMA50) is above the red line (SMA200) and otherwise out of the market else.

Strategy definition: Market timing price>SMA200

Name	MT-SPY-SMA-200
Assets	SPY
Simulation period	1/1/2000-1/1/2013
Re-balanced	Daily
Positions	1
Maximum Size	100%
Rules	Price > 200-day SMA
Leverage	1
Transactions costs	0
Benchmark	S&P 500 Index

The following simulations are performed from 1/1/2000 to 1/1/2013 (13 years).

The strategy returns data is in red, the blue one is SPY as a benchmark. Dividends are included in both charts. In these first examples, the position is examined daily and trading fees are not taken into account.

Chart 2.2: simulation of MT-SPY-SMA-200

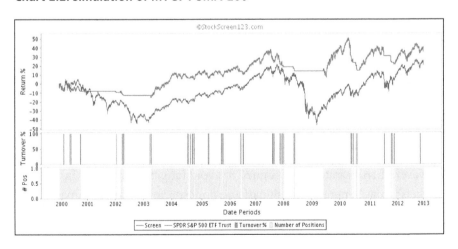

Strategy definition: Market timing SMA50>SMA200

Name	MT-SPY-SMA-50-200
Assets	SPY
Simulation period	1/1/2000-1/1/2013
Re-balanced	Daily
Positions	1
Maximum Size	100%
Rules	50-day SMA > 200-day SMA
Leverage	1
Transactions costs	0
Benchmark	S&P 500 Index

Chart 2.3: simulation of MT-SPY-SMA-50-200

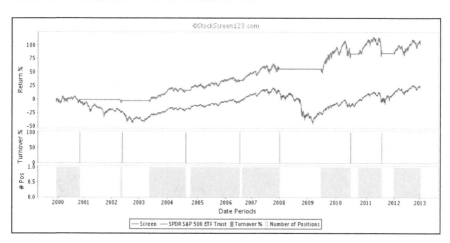

The second strategy based on two SMAs seems not only to give a better result than the first one, but to generate less trades.

However, such a strategy is designed to avoid long bear markets. In trending markets it may generate false signals and underperform the benchmark. It did since 2009.

Chart 2.4: simulation of MT-SPY-SMA-50-200 since 2009

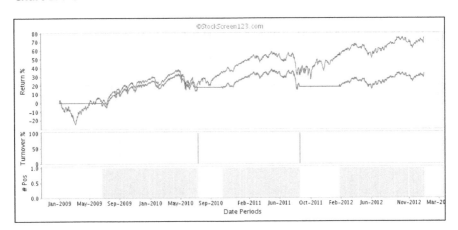

The good news is that even in this underperforming period (since 2009), the drawdown and volatility were kept lower than a buy-and-hold position.

The major advantage of being out of the market when SMA50 is below SMA200 is less to increase the return than to avoid the periods with the highest volatility and drawdowns. It opens the possibility to leverage our positions.

Strategy definition: Market timing SMA50>SMA200 2x leverage

Name	MT-SPY-SMA-50-200-X2
Assets	SPY
Simulation period	1/1/2000-1/1/2013
Re-balanced	Daily
Positions	1
Maximum Size	100%
Rules	50-day SMA > 200-day SMA
Leverage	2
Transactions costs	0
Benchmark	S&P 500 Index

Here is the chart of the double SMA market timing, with 2x leveraging:

Chart 2.5: Simulation of MT-SPY-SMA-50-200-X2

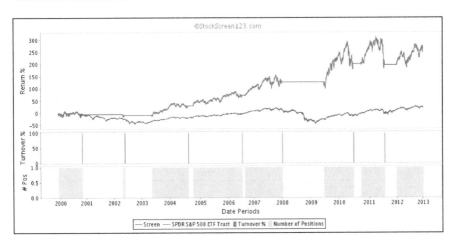

This table compares the total return, CAGR and maximum drawdown of the previous 13-year simulations:

Table 2.1: SPY strategies using SMAs

SPY	Total Return	CAGR	DDM
Buy & Hold	25.9	1.8	-55.4
MT-SPY-SMA-200	40.8	2.7	-24.2
MT-SPY-SMA-50-200	109.3	5.8	-17.0
MT-SPY-SMA-50-200-X2	275.0	10.7	-31.7

The lazy investor may be seduced by the last line in this table. About 9% a year above the buy-and-hold benchmark, with a much lower maximum drawdown, and only 15 trades in 13 years: this strategy looks not so bad. But this book will unveil better and safer ones.

You may wonder if market timing remains profitable if the moving averages and price are not checked every day.

The following table gives the returns and max drawdowns depending on the market timing frequency checking: every day, every week, every 4 weeks. For the latter I have simulated four starting dates: 1/1/2000, 1/8/2000, 1/15/2000 and 1/22/2000. It is necessary because a 4-week rebalancing may be very sensitive to the starting date.

Table 2.2: MT-SPY-SMA-50-200-X2 with different rebalancing periods and starting dates

Rebalancing	Total Return	CAGR	DDM
daily	275.0	10.7	-31.7
weekly	288.0	11.0	-33.0
4weeks 1/1	228.4	9.6	-37.6
4weeks 1/8	250.2	10.1	-39.5
4weeks 1/15	171.5	8.0	-35.0
4weeks 1/22	176.3	8.2	-36.9

The strategy has returns and drawdowns far better than buy-and-hold on all time scales. The difference between a daily and a weekly monitoring is not significant, however the 4-week rebalancing makes the results much more sensitive to the starting date and degrades significantly the drawdown and/or the return.

To make the results more realistic, I have run the simulation again with a 2% borrowing rate for the leveraged part, and a 0.1% rate for trading costs. Then in the case of a weekly checking, the CAGR is 9.4% and the drawdown 34%.

LONGER PERIODS

You may object that 13 years is quite a short period in financial market history.

Are we sure that market timing really works?

From a historical point of view, betting on this is reasonable. Some studies suggest that the results of a SMA200-based market timing is better in the very long term than between January 2000 and January 2013.

Here are numbers for the S&P 500 Index (including dividends) from 1900 to 2008 taken from the article "A Quantitative Approach to Tactical Asset Allocation" by Mebane Faber (2009):

Table 2.3: S&P 500 with dividends

S&P 500 w/div.	CAGR	DDM	Volatility	Sharpe
Buy & Hold	9.2	-83.7	17.9	0.29
Market Timing	10.5	-50.3	12.0	0.54

Faber's hypotheses are very close to mine, but there are differences. His SMA monitoring is monthly and his condition is that the price must be above the 10-month SMA (which is close to SMA200 in a daily time scale). In fact there is a high probability for the results with a double SMA and a weekly monitoring to be better.

These numbers suggest that in the very long term the CAGR is much better than it is since 2000: above 10% a year without leveraging. They also suggest that leveraging is not bulletproof: it would not have survived the 1929 crisis with a drawdown of 50%.

So if leveraging is not reasonable, why bother with market timing to make only 1.24% a year above buy-and-hold?

The answer is in the drawdown. In a 1929-like crisis, you might need to withdraw some money from your portfolio. It would be much easier if it is down "only" 50% from its highest point, not 83%.

And in the case where you lose your position by leveraging? Respecting Kelly's criterion (previously calculated), it would have been limited to less than 6% of your investments.

The first time I wrote an educational article on this subject, a reader made a disillusioned comment:

> Given any squiggly line, with perfect hind-sight you can develop some rule to capture its upside. But that says NOTHING about the value of the rule to capture up-side in the future.

My answer:

> If you have something to predict the future please don't tell us. Let me be happy when an anomaly gives a positive alpha on average since 1900. Human nature doesn't change, neither do the behaviors driving the market.

MULTI-INDEXES TIMING

A PORTFOLIO OF 5 U.S. STOCK INDEXES

U.S. stock indexes are strongly correlated but not equal. In this part the idea is to create a portfolio with:

- Dow Jones Industrial Average [DIA],

- S&P 500 [SPY],

- NASDAQ 100 [QQQ],

- S&P Midcap 400 [MDY], and

- Russell 2000 [IWM].

(The symbols for their respective ETFs are in the square brackets.)

An equal weight portfolio of those 5 index ETFs has outperformed SPY by about 2% a year from January 2000 to January 2013 (dividends are included).

Strategy definition: Buy and hold five indices

Name	BH-5ind
Assets	DIA, SPY, QQQ, MDY, IWM
Simulation period	1/1/2000-1/1/2013
Re-balanced	Annually
Positions	5
Maximum Size	20%
Rules	Buy and Hold
Leverage	1
Transactions costs	0.1%
Benchmark	S&P 500 Index

Chart 2.6: Simulation of BH-5ind

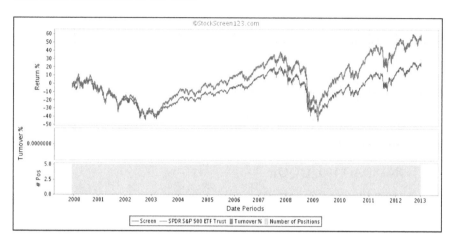

It is not sensitive to the rebalancing period: from a daily to a yearly rebalancing, the CAGR remains between 3.65% and 3.75% (vs 1.79% for SPY alone), and the drawdown between -54.1% and -54.6%.

The idea is now to apply the previous double SMA market timing rule in two different ways:

1. *Individually*. I check the condition for each ETF once a week starting 1/1/2000. If an ETF is considered as bearish for the rule (SMA50 <= SMA200), this ETF position is converted to cash. It is bought again when SMA50>SMA200. Each position is limited to 20% of the portfolio value.

2. *Globally*. The market timing rule is checked on the S&P 500 index and all ETFs are sold and bought together.

Strategy definition: Individual market timing on five indices

Name	MTindiv-5ind
Assets	DIA, SPY, QQQ, MDY, IWM
Simulation period	1/1/2000-1/1/2013
Re-balanced	weekly
Positions	0 to 5
Maximum Size	20%
Rules	50-day SMA > 200-day SMA
Leverage	1
Transactions costs	0.1%
Benchmark	S&P 500 Index

Strategy definition: Global market timing on five indices

Name	MTglobal-5ind
Assets	DIA, SPY, QQQ, MDY, IWM
Simulation period	1/1/2000-1/1/2013
Re-balanced	weekly
Positions	0 or 5
Maximum Size	20%
Rules	(50-day SMA > 200-day SMA) for SPY
Leverage	1
Transactions costs	0.1%
Benchmark	S&P 500 Index

The following table gives the numbers from 13-year simulations starting 1/1/2000.

Table 2.4: 5 U.S. stock indexes with two SMAs

Strategy	Total Return	CAGR	DDM
BH-5ind	61.3	3.8	-54.2
MTindiv-5ind	64.4	3.9	-26.3
MTglobal-5ind	140.1	7.0	-17.9

Whereas the individual market timing cuts by 48% (from 54.18% to 26.30%) the maximum drawdown without touching significantly the return, the simpler global market timing reduces the drawdown by more than 60% and doubles the annual return.

This is a case where making things simpler may improve the performance and reduce the risk.

If you try to compute the Kelly criterion, you will obtain a value very similar to the previous example. It doesn't mean that you can invest 6% of your money on the S&P 500 and 6% on a five-index portfolio with the same (or a similar) market timing rule. It is just a variant of the same game of market-timing on US stocks. Betting twice the amount on the same game would increase the probability of ruin and break Kelly's philosophy.

SECTOR PORTFOLIO TIMING

What about applying the same idea to sectors?

Among the possible candidates, I propose the 11 most liquid sector ETFs from the iShares series:

Table 2.5: 11 sector ETFs

Ticker	ETF Name	Inception
IYM	iShares Dow Jones US Basic Materials	June 2000
IYC	iShares Dow Jones US Consumer Services	June 2000
IYK	iShares Dow Jones US Consumer Goods	June 2000
IYE	iShares Dow Jones US Energy	June 2000
IYF	iShares Dow Jones US Financial Sector	May 2000
IYH	iShares Dow Jones US Healthcare	June 2000
IYJ	iShares Dow Jones US Industrial	June 2000
IYR	iShares Dow Jones US Real Estate	June 2000
IYW	iShares Dow Jones US Technology	May 2000
IYZ	iShares Dow Jones US Telecom	May 2000
IDU	iShares Dow Jones US Utilities	June 2000

Because of the start dates and the need to have 200 days of data to calculate SMA200, in this part the simulations are from 6/1/2001 to 1/1/2013.

This time, I will apply the double SMA market timing rule in three ways:

1. Strategy definition: Individual market timing on 11 sectors

I check the condition for each ETF once a week starting 6/1/2001. If SMA50 <= SMA200 the position is cash. It is bought again when SMA50>SMA200. Each position is limited to 1/11 of the portfolio value.

Name	MTindiv-11sectors
Assets	IYM, IYC, IYK, IYE, IYF, IYH, IYJ, IYR, IYW, IYZ, IDU
Simulation period	6/1/2001-1/1/2013
Re-balanced	weekly
Positions	0 to 11
Maximum Size	9.1%
Rules	50-day SMA > 200-day SMA
Leverage	1
Transactions costs	0.1%
Benchmark	S&P 500 Index

2. Strategy definition: Global market timing on 11 sectors

The market timing rule is checked on the S&P 500 index and all ETFs are sold and bought together.

Name	MTglobal-11sectors
Assets	IYM, IYC, IYK, IYE, IYF, IYH, IYJ, IYR, IYW, IYZ, IDU
Simulation period	6/1/2001-1/1/2013
Re-balanced	weekly
Positions	0 or 11
Maximum Size	9.1%
Rules	(50-day SMA > 200-day SMA) for SPY
Leverage	1
Transactions costs	0.1%
Benchmark	S&P 500 Index

3. Strategy definition: Combining Individual and Global rule, and cancelling the 1/11 constraint

It means that the portfolio is out of the market if SMA50 <= SMA200 for the S&P500 index. Else, the individual rule is checked for every ETF. The portfolio is equal-weight on the ETFs for which SMA50>SMA200, without limit of percentage.

Name	MTcomb-11sectors
Assets	IYM, IYC, IYK, IYE, IYF, IYH, IYJ, IYR, IYW, IYZ, IDU
Simulation period	6/1/2001-1/1/2013
Re-balanced	weekly
Positions	0 to 11
Maximum Size	100%
Rules	(50-day SMA > 200-day SMA) for SPY and 50-day SMA > 200-day SMA
Leverage	1
Transactions costs	0.1%
Benchmark	S&P 500 Index

Here are the results, compared with buy-and-hold, and the previous cases reconsidered on this shorter period.

Table 2.6: Comparison of market timing strategies with SPY, 5 indexes, 11 sectors

Strategy	Total Return	CAGR	DDM
SPY Buy & Hold	43.9	3.2	-55.4
MT-SPY-SMA-50-200	116.9	6.9	-17.2
MTglobal-5ind	137.6	7.8	-19.5
11 sectors Buy & Hold	82.1	5.3	-55.7
MTindiv-11sectors	102.1	6.3	-17.3
MTglobal-11sectors	148.8	8.2	-17.5
MTcomb-11sectors	160.0	8.6	-17

The global timing is superior in return to the individual timing on the period, and here the combined version is even slightly better.

The same remark as in the previous part applies here: this is just an improved variant of the initial SPY market timing. Don't consider it as a different strategy for Kelly's criterion. The following part *is* different because it introduces less correlated asset classes.

GLOBAL ASSETS PORTFOLIO TIMING

Now let us consider investing in three asset classes:

- treasury bonds
- global stocks
- real estate

Treasury bonds can be sub-divided regarding their terms, and stocks regarding the region of the world. I have chosen a set of 7 ETFs:

Table 2.7: 7 global assets ETFs

Ticker	Name	Inception
IEF	iShares Barclays 7-10 Year Treasury	July 2002
TLT	iShares Barclays 20+ Year Treas Bond	July 2002
SPY	SPDR S&P 500	Jan 1993
IEV	iShares S&P Europe 350 Index	July 2000
ILF	iShares S&P Latin America 40 Index	Oct 2001
EPP	iShares MSCI Pacific ex-Japan	Oct 2001
ICF	iShares Cohen & Steers Realty Majors	Jan 2001

Because of the inception dates and our requirement for the calculation of the SMA200, the simulations are performed from 6/1/2003 to 1/1/2013. That is 9.5 years.

The following tables shows two variants of applying weekly the double SMA market timing rule individually to each ETF.

1. Strategy definition: with a limit of ⅐ of the portfolio value for every position

Name	MT-7assets-limited
Assets	IEF, TLT, SPY, IEV, ILF, EPP, ICF
Simulation period	6/1/2003-1/1/2013
Re-balanced	weekly
Positions	0 to 7
Maximum Size	14.3%
Rules	50-day SMA > 200-day SMA
Leverage	1
Transactions costs	0
Benchmark	S&P 500 Index

2. Strategy definition: no limit

Name	MT-7assets-unlimited
Assets	IEF, TLT, SPY, IEV, ILF, EPP, ICF
Simulation period	6/1/2003-1/1/2013
Re-balanced	weekly
Positions	0 to 7
Maximum Size	100%
Rules	50-day SMA > 200-day SMA
Leverage	1
Transactions costs	0
Benchmark	S&P 500 Index

There is also a comparison with buy-and-hold and the previous strategies on the reduced time interval.

Table 2.8: 7 global assets using two SMAs

Strategy	Total Return	CAGR	DDM
SPYBuy & Hold	80.6	6.4	-55.4
MT-SPY-SMA-50-200	111.0	8.1	-17.2
MTglobal-5ind	127.3	8.9	-19.5
MTcomb-11sectors	154.2	10.2	-17.3
7 assets Buy & Hold	195.0	11.9	-45.8
MT-7assets-limited	180.1	11.3	-11.4
MT-7assets-unlimited	272.1	14.7	-17.9

Even the buy-and-hold version has a better return that any previous strategy, but the drawdown is still high. The market timing with limited position keeps the return in the same range and divides by four the maximum drawdown.

The unlimited version improves the average return at the price of a higher drawdown.

Here is a more realistic and detailed comparison of both versions. A 0.1% rate is applied for the trading fees and a 2% rate for borrowing in the leveraged versions.

Table 2.9: global assets market timing strategies, unleveraged and leveraged twice

Strategy	Total Return	CAGR	DDM	Sortino	Kelly	Sterling	DD-lengthMax
MT-7assets-limited	176.6	11.2	-11.4	0.84	0.20	0.52	90 weeks
MT-7assets-unlimited	265.6	14.5	-18.0	0.88	0.19	0.52	88 weeks
MT-7assets-limited-X2	522.5	21.0	-21.9	0.96	0.19	0.66	91 weeks
MT-7assets-unlimited-X2	811.3	25.9	-34.5	0.90	0.18	0.58	88 weeks

The most aggressive investors will be seduced by the unlimited leveraged version which has the highest CAGR. The most conservative ones will stick to the unleveraged limited version which has the lowest drawdown and the highest Kelly ratio.

Objectively, the best risk-adjusted performance is obtained with the limited leverage, because it has the highest Sortino and Sterling ratios.

Here is the corresponding simulation chart.

Chart 2.7: Simulation of MT-7assets-limited-X2

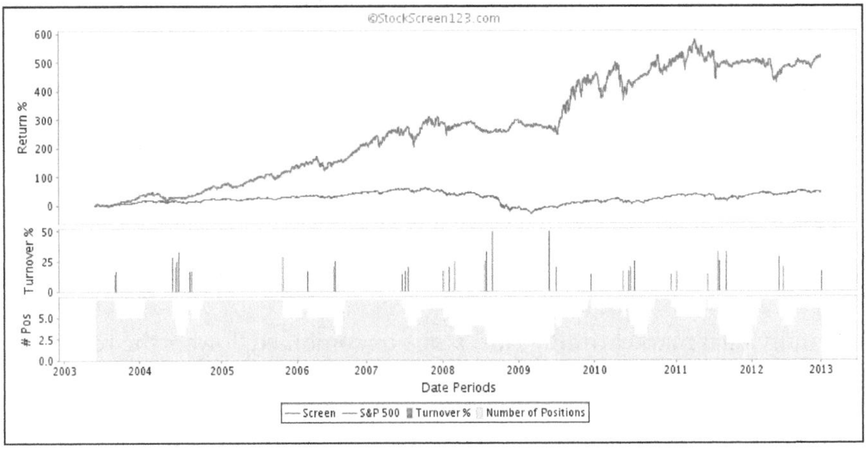

> **Note**
>
> I wrote in the introduction chapter that the Kelly criterion was an invariant by leveraging. This property is lost after applying trading costs and borrowing rates.
>
> If you are not confident in the relatively short time period of simulation (a little bit less than 10 years), please note that in the article quoted previously M. Faber has simulated a similar strategy on asset class indexes from 1973 to 2008. His unleveraged CAGR is above 11% and his drawdown below 10%. There are two major differences between his model and mine: I have not included commodities and my model emphasizes stocks, both in regional diversification and in relative weight.

Individual stock timing

Let's apply the individual, global and combined market timing rules to the 500 stocks of the S&P 500 universe, just as I did for sector ETFs. Each position is limited to $\frac{1}{500}$ of the portfolio.

The following table gives the results with a weekly rebalancing from 1/1/2000 to 1/1/2013. A 0.1% rate for trading costs is applied.

Table 2.10: S&P 500 individual stocks using two SMAs

	Total Return	CAGR	DDM
SPY Buy & Hold	25.9	1.8	-55.4
S&P Universe Buy & Hold	153.3	7.4	-57.9
S&P Universe Individual MT	94.5	5.3	-20.7
S&P Universe Global MT	179.6	8.2	-22.4
S&P Universe Combined MT	122.8	6.4	-16.3

The individual market timing rule, alone or combined, lowers the return.

The global market timing alone gives the best return, and the combined version shows the lowest drawdown.

Don't be surprised that the universe buy-and-hold return is different from SPY: the simulated portfolio is equal-weight, the S&P 500 index and SPY are not. If you want an equal weight S&P 500 ETF, have a look at RSP (Rydex S&P 500 Equal Weight).

CONCLUSION

The double SMA market timing rules also works on stocks. Additional rules may be added to build really profitable strategies.

As previously on indexes and sectors:

- The main effect is to drastically lower the drawdown.

- Simpler is better: a global MT rule on the index gives a higher return.

CHAPTER SUMMARY

- Market timing is presented through basic rules using 50-day and 200-day simple moving averages.

- A few ETF strategies are presented on U.S. stock indexes, sectors and global assets.

- Among them, the most profitable strategy during the last decade was on global assets.

- References to publications using a much longer timescale are given as an indication that these kind of strategies might be relatively safe for a long term investor.

- The same rules are applied to the set of all individual stocks of the S&P 500 index. The conclusion is that trading sectors or assets globally gives better performances.

CHAPTER 3:

MOMENTUM

WE HAVE SEEN IN CHAPTER 1 that the word "momentum" designates either the return of an asset on a specified time interval, or the ratio between the final and the initial price on this interval. It is an indicator of trend. When using it here to rank assets, we have also seen that both calculation methods are equivalent.

Basically there are two ways to make money on the long side: buy low to sell high (what everybody tries to do first), and buy high to sell higher (what a lot of people do after losing money the first way).

Following trends is more comfortable and predictable. I will now illustrate this using the sector and assets ETF sets defined previously. This chapter will also introduce a specific, simple and efficient category of momentum strategies called *paired switching*.

SECTOR ROTATION

When setting up a momentum ETF strategy for sectors, two questions must be answered:

1. how many periods for the momentum, and
2. how many positions in the portfolio?

Previous studies and publications have shown that almost any momentum between 20 trading days and 1 year (~250 trading days) is acceptable for the long term for U.S. sectors.

For the number of positions, we have the choice between keeping the best sectors or eliminating the worst from the momentum ranking.

Choosing a momentum: I propose to start from the combined market timing strategy on sectors and to keep only the top 6 sectors ranked on 20-day, 60-day, 120-day and 200-day momentum. The following table shows the results and compares them with the combined market timing on the whole set as a benchmark.

Table 3.1: top 6 sectors, always with combined market timing

6/1/2001-1/1/2013	Total Return	CAGR	DDM
11 sectors, combined MT	165.5	8.8	-17.3
Top 6 Momentum 200	154.6	8.4	-18.2
Top 6 Momentum 120	167.7	8.9	-16.9
Top 6 Momentum 60	146.3	8.1	-16.6
Top 6 Momentum 20	195.4	9.8	-16.0

The 20-day momentum gives a higher return and a lower drawdown. Please note that there is no attempt of optimization here: I test only plain intervals. Moreover there is no risk of over-fitting: they all give a CAGR between 8% and 10%.

CHOOSING THE NUMBER OF POSITIONS

Now, let's explore how the results vary with the maximum number of positions.

Table 3.2: 20-day momentum, combined market timing

6/1/2001-1/1/2013	Total Return	CAGR	DDM
Top 1	3.6	0.3	-29.5
Top 2	96.3	6.0	-22.7
Top 3	137.4	7.7	-20.3
Top 4	167.0	8.8	-17.2
Top 5	181.8	9.4	-16.9
Top 6	195.4	9.8	-16.0
Top 7	192.5	9.7	-17.2
Top 8	177.4	9.2	-17.5
Top 9	184.2	9.4	-17.3
Top 10	170.2	9.0	-17.6

I wrote "maximum" because in the top N choice, the number of actual positions in the portfolio is N *or less* after checking the individual market timing rule.

When keeping the top 4 or more, the return and the drawdown are similar or better than the 11-sector benchmark. The results are quite stable between 4 and 11 positions, which is a good thing: it shows that there is little risk that the choice of momentum interval is over-fitted to the behaviour of particular sectors during the simulation period.

There is a sweet point at 6: this is the highest return and the best drawdown (for the drawdown, lower is better in absolute value). However, the additional gain is not large: just 1% in return and 1.3% in drawdown over the 11-sector benchmark.

In fact, performance can still be improved.

ENHANCING PERFORMANCE WITH BONDS

Don't forget that the portfolio is out of the market when SMA50<=SMA200 on the S&P 500 index. This is the global market timing rule. Instead of cash, the strategy could invest in a bond ETF during this time.

I propose to use IEF (iShares Barclays 7-10 Year Treasury). As its start month was July 2002, the simulation period has to be reduced by 1 year and 2 months.

Here is a comparison of the strategy without, and with IEF. To make it realistic, a 0.1% rate for the transaction costs is applied. Remember that all these ETFs are very liquid.

Table 3.3: Top 6 sectors, 20-day Momentum, Combined Market Timing

8/1/2002-1/1/2013	Total Return	CAGR	DDM	Sortino	Kelly	Sterling	DD-lengthMax
Top 6	152.0	9.3	-16.2	0.47	0.16	0.35	88 weeks
Top 6 w/IEF	234.9	12.3	-16.2	0.79	0.17	0.47	62 weeks

Adding IEF greatly improves the return, the Sortino ratio and the length of drawdown duration.

Strategy definition: Top 6 sectors for a 20-day momentum, with combined market timing and IEF

Name	Sectors-Top6-IEF
Assets	IEF, IYM, IYC, IYK, IYE, IYF, IYH, IYJ, IYR, IYW, IYZ, IDU
Simulation period	8/1/2002-1/1/2013
Re-balanced	weekly
Positions	1 to 6
Maximum Size	100%
Rules	If (50-day SMA <= 200-day SMA) for SPY, then select IEF; Else list the 6 sector ETFs with the highest 20-day Momentum and select these for which 50-day SMA > 200-day SMA
Leverage	1
Transactions costs	0.1%
Benchmark	S&P 500 Index

Here is the simulation chart:

Chart 3.1: Simulation for Sectors-Top6-IEF

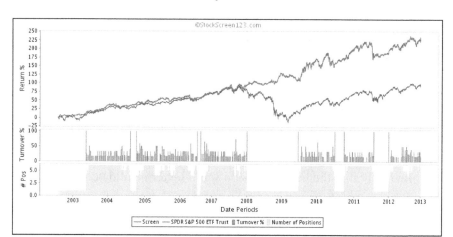

We can note that the individual timing applies after all other rules, whatever the selection: equities or bonds. It explains why the portfolio is completely out of the market during a short period in 2006. SMA50 was below SMA200 for the S&P 500 and for IEF at the same time.

Remember also that according to the previous chapter, there is no limit in size position. For example if the global market timing is bullish for equities, and if 6 sectors are selected by the momentum, but only 4 pass the individual timing, then the portfolio has 4 positions of 25% each. If the global market timing is bearish, the whole portfolio is invested in the bond ETF.

CHANGING THE REBALANCING PERIOD

If a weekly checking is too much work, the strategy works also on a 4-week rebalancing with diminished performance. Depending on the starting date, the minimum CAGR is 10.5% and the maximum drawdown -22.5%.

GLOBAL ASSETS ROTATION

After the trial on sectors, let's do the same with the next set of ETFs (global assets).

The first step is to explore the numbers for different momentum lengths with an arbitrary number of assets.

CHOOSING A MOMENTUM

Keeping roughly half of the pack as I did for sectors is not enough in my opinion. In this case I prefer to eliminate just one and keep also the top 6. We saw previously that the limited version was a better candidate for leveraging (keeping a limit of $\frac{1}{7}$ for each portfolio position). I propose to continue in the same way: for the top 6 momentum portfolio, I fix the position size limit to $\frac{1}{6}$ of the portfolio value at each rebalancing.

Table 3.4: Top 6 global assets with different momentums, limited position size. Always with market timing.

6/1/2003-1/1/2013	Total Return	CAGR	DDM
MT-7assets-limited	180.1	11.3	-11.4
Top 6 Momentum 200	215.3	12.7	-12.5
Top 6 Momentum 120	230.6	13.3	-11.8
Top 6 Momentum 60	205.8	12.4	-12.4
Top 6 Momentum 20	145.1	9.8	-11.8

In this case, a longer momentum gives a better performance. The top 6 gives a better return than the benchmark on a wide range of momentum periods, at least from 60 days to 200 days. The maximum among the tested values is at 120 trading days (about 6 months).

CHOOSING THE NUMBER OF POSITIONS

Now, let's test the maximum size of portfolio:

Table 3.5: top N global assets for a 120-day momentum, N from 1 to 6. Position size limited to 1/N

6/1/2003-1/1/2013	Total Return	CAGR	DDM
Top 1 limited	553.4	21.6	-28.3
Top 2 limited	321.6	16.2	-23.7
Top 3 limited	330.0	16.4	-19.1
Top 4 limited	298.9	15.5	-15.2
Top 5 limited	292.6	15.3	-13.7
Top 6 limited	230.6	13.3	-11.8

In contrast to the sectors, selecting the best ranked ETF gives the best return. Considering the possibility of leveraging, we have already seen that the best return may not be the best strategy. From this point of view, the Top 5 shows very good characteristics.

The drawdown is lower than the CAGR. An average return above 15% makes it a profitable strategy, and a drawdown below 14% makes leveraging possible for an aggressive investor.

Here is a detailed comparison of the leveraged and non-leveraged versions, and I have included the best choice with an unlimited position size, which is the top 4 assets (also based on a 120-day momentum).

Table 3.6: Variations on Top N global assets

6/1/2003-1/1/2013	Total Return	CAGR	DDM	Sortino	Kelly	Sterling	DD-length Max
Top 5 limited	277.1	14.9	-13.7	0.96	0.20	0.63	88 weeks
Top 5 limited leveraged x2	943.9	27.7	-26.2	1.03	0.19	0.76	91 weeks
Top 4 unlimited	331.1	16.5	-17.9	0.94	0.18	0.59	88 weeks

A Sortino ratio close to 1 and a Kelly ratio close to 0.2 are signs of robust strategies, provided that the simulation is long enough and covers bull and bear markets. The higher these values, the better.

Strategy definition: Top 5 assets for a 120-day momentum, leveraged twice

Name	Assets-Top5 x2
Assets	IEF, TLT, SPY, IEV, ILF, EPP, ICF
Simulation period	6/1/2003-1/1/2013
Re-balanced	weekly
Positions	0 to 5
Maximum Size	20%
Rules	List the 5 ETFs with the highest 120-day Momentum and select these for which 50-day SMA > 200-day SMA
Leverage	2
Transactions costs	0.1%
Benchmark	S&P 500 Index

Here is the chart for the Top 5 limited leveraged version.

Chart 3.2: simulation of Assets-Top5-Leveraged twice

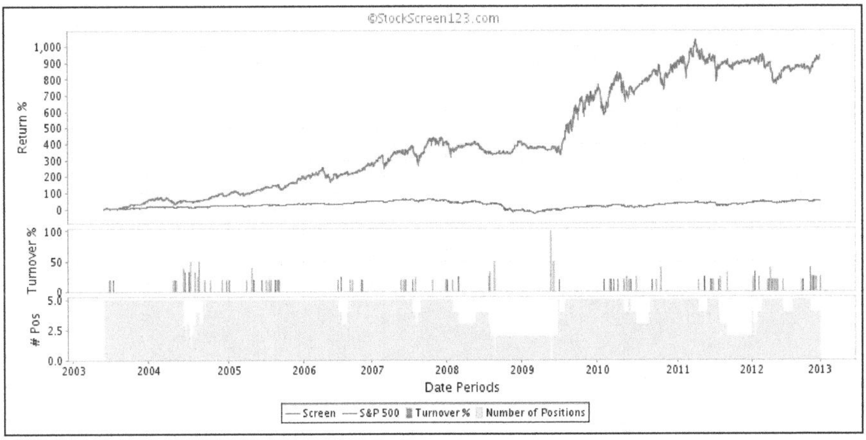

It also works on a monthly basis. Testing a 4-week rebalancing with 4 successive starting weeks, the minimum CAGR is 25.5% and the maximum drawdown -31%.

PAIRED SWITCHING

Paired switching refers to investing in two negatively correlated assets on the basis of their recent performance or any other appropriate criterion. The evaluation of the criterion and the decision to switch or not is generally taken monthly or quarterly.

Paired switching is fundamentally different from pairs-trading, which deals with two correlated (or *cointegrated*) assets and tries to exploit discrepancies in their behavior.

When the criterion for paired switching is the total return for a recent period (or a combination of total returns on recent periods), it falls into the category of momentum strategy.

CHOOSING TWO ETFS

The easiest way to implement paired switching is to take a stock index ETF and a T-Bond ETF as negatively correlated assets. The following table shows simulation results with TLT as the bond ETF, 5 different stock index ETFs and the following hypotheses:

Strategy definition: Paired switching for a 60-day momentum with TLT and various stock indices

- One position in portfolio
- The portfolio is long the ETF with the highest return over last 60 trading days
- Rebalanced every 4 weeks starting 8/1/2002
- 0.1% trading costs

Name	PairedSwitching-Index-TLT
Assets	One index ETF and TLT
Simulation period	8/1/2002-1/1/2013
Re-balanced	4-week
Positions	1
Maximum Size	100%
Rules	Select the ETF with the highest 60-day Momentum between TLT and the index ETF Leverage 1
Transactions costs	0.1%
Benchmark	S&P 500 Index

Table 3.7: Results of PairedSwitching-Index-TLT with different index ETFs

Index ETF	Total Return	CAGR	DDM	Sortino
DIA	188.9	10.7	-16.9	0.65
SPY	231.8	12.2	-17.7	0.74
QQQ	243.8	12.6	-32.0	0.67
MDY	463.9	18.1	-22.9	1.12
IWM	399.0	16.7	-23.7	0.92

Once again we see that all indexes are not equal. The strategy using the midcap ETF MDY has an impressive performance: a return above 15% and a Sortino ratio above 1 are very good, especially for a very simple strategy.

Over the same period, the annualized return of holding MDY and TLT (without switching) were respectively 9.89% and 8.14%, with maximum drawdowns of -55.37% and -27%. As a monthly strategy may be very sensitive to starting dates, I have tested it with four starting dates separated by a one-week interval. The detailed statistics are not very useful here, but it is interesting to note that the return stays between 17.8% and 22%, and the drawdown between 18 and 27%. According to my experience with thousands of simulations, these are quite stable results for a 4-week rebalancing. Most monthly strategies are more sensitive to the starting date.

EMERGING MARKETS

Now I propose to play again with an ETF on emerging countries: EEM.

By definition, what is emerging is supposed to have better growth prospects than the global benchmark. This is an additional bias. EEM's holdings in 5, 10 or 20 years will probably not be the same as today. Most indices and ETFs are dynamic. But EEM has the specifity to look all over the world for growing companies in growing economies. In the future, new countries will emerge, and emerging countries will reach the developed category. Should I also replace the T-bond ETF (TLT) by an emerging sovereign bond ETF (for example PCY or EMB)?

The answer is: absolutely not. The emerging debt is a valuable asset in a global portfolio, but it is positively correlated with stocks and doesn't suit our goals.

The following table shows simulation results with the following hypotheses:

- from 5/1/2003 (because of EEM start date) to 2/15/2013
- the ETF with the highest return last 60 days is chosen
- rebalancing every 4 weeks
- 0.1% trading costs.

As it is a monthly strategy, 4 starting dates at least must be tested.

Table 3.8: Variations of PairedSwitching-Index-TLT with EEM as index ETF, different starting dates

EEM/TLT	Total Return	CAGR	DDM	Sortino
05/01/03	728.7	24.1	-29.5	1.13
05/08/03	710.6	23.9	-31.1	1.19
05/15/03	507.7	20.3	-27.7	0.98
05/22/03	540.3	21.0	-23.9	1.02

For the same period, the CAGR of holding EEM and TLT were respectively 16.2% and 7.2%, with maximum drawdowns of -64.3% and -27%.

Therefore, the strategy significantly improves the return of just holding EEM and transforms an unacceptable drawdown to a reasonable one.

Caution: specialized stock ETFs are not good candidates for paired-switching. For example it works better with multi-sectorial ETFs like MDY and EEM than with sector ETFs.

The Triple Switch variant

This is the same as paired-switching, except that you make your choice among three ETFs.

I propose an example using TLT, MDY and EEM with the same hypotheses as the previous simulation:

Strategy definition: Triple switch for a 60-day momentum with MDY, EEM and TLT

- 5/1/2003 to 2/15/2013
- the ETF with the highest return last 60 days is chosen
- rebalancing every 4 weeks
- 0.1% trading costs

Name	TripleSwitch
Assets	MDY, EEM, TLT
Simulation period	5/1/2003-1/1/2013
Re-balanced	4-week
Positions	1
Maximum Size	100%
Rules	Select the ETF with the highest 60-day Momentum
Leverage	1
Transactions costs	0.1%
Benchmark S&P 500	Index

The following table shows a summary of simulations with 4 starting dates:

Table 3.9: Variations of TripleSwitch for different starting dates

Triple Switch	Total Return	CAGR	DDM	Sortino
01/05/03	1059.6	28.4	-30.9	1.40
08/05/03	939.7	27.1	-28.5	1.45
15/05/03	800.2	25.3	-26.1	1.31
22/05/03	1101.5	29.1	-23.9	1.50

Here are the detailed results with the first starting date:

Table 3.10: Detailed results for TripleSwitch

Criteria	Value
Total Return	1059.6%
CAGR	28.4%
Maximum Drawdown Depth	-30.9%
Maximum Drawdown duration	21 months
Sortino Ratio	1.4
Average 4-week gain	4.7% (2-digit precision)
Average 4-week loss	-3.7% (2-digit precision)
Experimental probability of gain (P)	68.5%
Statistical probability of gain with a 95% confidence interval (P95)	60% – it means that the real probability has a 95% chance to be above 60%.
Kelly criterion	44% (or 27% using P95)

To summarize, the triple switch has very good statistical characteristics, but a maximum drawdown duration of almost two years may be an obstacle for investors with mid-term goals.

CONCLUSION

A conclusion about double and triple switches: as long as stocks and bonds are negatively correlated, these strategies should continue to outperform both classes of asset in the long term. It doesn't matter if stocks or bonds are in a bull or bear market. Paired switching is symmetric and designed to capture the best of both worlds. Nevertheless, past results are never a guarantee for the future.

For Individual Stocks?

To evaluate the idea on stocks, I start from the combined market timing applied on the S&P 500 universe, as it is described at the end of Chapter 2 (Individual Stock Timing). Then I select the top 100 stocks in a momentum ranking. The position size is limited to 1%, and a 0.2% rate is applied for spread and trading fees. Here is the result for the usual momentum lengths. The benchmark is a combined market timing applied to the whole universe (see previous chapter).

Table 3.11: Top 100 stocks from S&P 500 index for different momentums with combined market timing rules

6/1/2001-1/1/2013	Total Return	CAGR	DDM
Benchmark:500 stocks MT	118.4	6.2	-16.5
Top 100 Momentum 200	84.9	4.8	-21.5
Top 100 Momentum 120	53.9	3.4	-26.8
Top 100 Momentum 60	40.5	2.7	-23.5
Top 100 Momentum 20	8.8	0.7	-24.4

It doesn't work here. The shorter the momentum, the lower the return.

CHAPTER SUMMARY

- Different momentum ETF strategies are presented on sectors and global assets.

- Variations on the momentum duration and number of selected ETFs are tested on 10-year simulations.

- The momentum ranking and selection is used as an addition to market timing.

- The best options use the top 6 sectors for a 20-day momentum and the top 5 global assets for a 120-day momentum.

- Bonds are used in combination with strategies on indices and sectors to enhance performance.

- Paired-switching and triple-switch are presented as simple and valuable alternatives of momentum strategies.

- The conclusion is negative about using the same methodology on individual S&P 500 stocks.

CHAPTER 4:

SEASONAL PATTERNS

THIS CHAPTER DEALS WITH THE THIRD CATEGORY of anomalies explored in this book: annual cycles. It begins with a presentation of the most recent academic research, then applies two-season and four-season patterns to diversified stock indexes. Then it focuses on what usually happens on the stock market at the end of the year. It also shows a strategy using two sectors and a three-season pattern. It ends with an overview of monthly patterns in all kinds of asset classes.

THE ONLY STRATEGY BACKTESTED OVER 319 YEARS

Most human activities have seasonal cycles. The stock market's seasonal cycle is not reliable every year, but it is powerful over the long term.

You have probably already heard of its four best-known effects:

1. **Sell in May and Go Away**: this old saying says that the odds are against you from May until Fall.

2. **Halloween Effect**: the odds are favorable again in November and a rally may take place just before Halloween. Sell in May and Halloween are the pivot points of the same annual cycle: the first one tells when to go out of the stock market, the second one when to step in again.

3. **Santa Claus Rally**: "A surge in the price of stocks that often occurs in the week between Christmas and New Year's Day." (Definition from Investopedia.com.)

4. **January Effect**: "Refers to the historical pattern that stock prices rise in the first few days of January. Studies have suggested this holds only for small-capitalization stocks." (Definition from Nasdaq.com.)

HALLOWEEN EFFECT

This section will look at just the Halloween Effect.

It is said that all the positive return of the stock market occurs during the 6-month period from the 1st of November to the 30th of April, and that it's better to be out of the market from the 1st of May to the 31st of October.

But is this just a legend or does it really work?

Lots of research articles have been published on the subject, generally with partial data and unconvincing explanations. Until recently there was no exhaustive study to prove that one of the best quantitative indicators might be the calendar.

Late in 2012, Ben Jacobsen and Cherry Y. Zhang from Massey University (New Zealand) wrote two unbelievable articles: 'Are Monthly Seasonals Real? A Three Century Perspective' and 'The Halloween Indicator: Everywhere and all the time'[1]. These are the lethal weapons against scepticism! Compiling data from 1693 in 108 countries, they claim that not only is the discrepancy between Summer and Winter as old as the availability of stock data, but that it can be observed worldwide and has increased in the last decades. I think that these academic papers are a must read for anyone seriously involved at any level in the stock market. In-depth statistics can be found in the original articles.

The following table shows monthly average returns in percentage from different sources. The first column is a summary of the most important numbers in Jacobsen & Zhang's papers, the second and the third columns are drawn from online data sources, the fourth one gives results obtained by my own analysis. Like Jacobsen I call "Winter" the 6 months from November to April and "Summer" the 6 months from May to September.

---

[1] Both papers available at the Social Science Research Network website (**www.ssrn.com**).

Table 4.1: monthly and seasonal average returns (%) for different periods since 1693

	316 years[1] 1693-2009	82 years[2] 1929-2011	50 years[2] 1961-2011	14 years[3] 1999-2012
January	0.69	1.00	1.20	-1.60
February	0.09	0.00	0.00	-1.30
March	-0.03	0.40	1.10	2.70
April	0.49	1.40	2.00	2.70
May	0.02	-0.20	-0.10	-0.80
June	-0.12	0.50	-0.60	-1.22
July	-0.31	1.50	0.90	0.34
August	0.44	0.80	0.20	0.39
September	-0.49	-1.30	-0.80	-1.28
October	-0.50	0.00	0.50	1.32
November	0.35	0.80	1.20	1.20
December	0.81	1.50	1.50	2.60
Winter	2.42	5.20	7.20	6.36
Summer	-0.96	1.28	0.09	-1.27
Whole Year	1.44	6.55	7.29	5.01
Difference W-S	3.38	3.92	7.11	7.63

[1]Jacobsen's Global Financial Data Index
[2]Dow Jones Industrial Average
[3]SPDR Dow Jones Industrial Average (DIA)

The best months of the year are April and December, joined by March in recent years. The months with the lowest returns are May, June and September. September is the only month to be negative on all four timeframes. Please note that January has been one of the best months in the past, and the worst one for at least 14 years. The least we can say is that the January effect didn't work well from 1999 to 2012: both big cap and small cap U.S. indexes have a negative average return for this month.

Jacobsen and Zhang have also noted that the U.S. stock market had historically one of the best average winter gains among developed countries.

The following charts show that since 1950 until 2011, being out of the market for 6 months from May to October would have avoided a 10% loss, and above all would have avoided major drawdowns. The complete data series can be found in the appendix.

The first two charts give the total return and drawdown of investing in DJIA every year from the 1st of November to the 30th of April, and being out of the market the rest of the year. Years are numbered from 1 (1950) to 61 (2011). The drawdown is measured at the end of the season. It means that the real time drawdown during a season can be worse than what is shown on the chart.

Chart 4.1: cumulative return of DJIA from November to April, 1950-2011

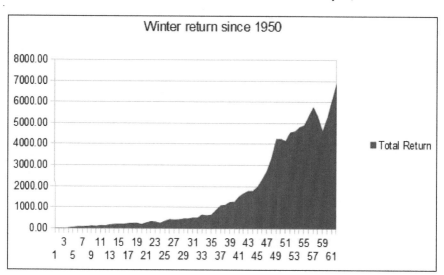

Chart 4.2: cumulative drawdown of DJIA from November to April, 1950-2011

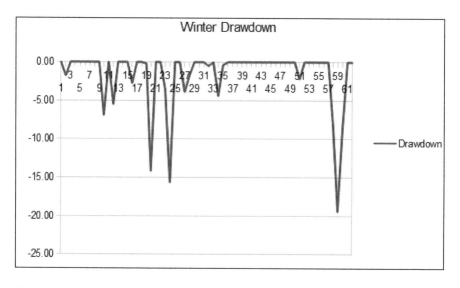

Now the total return and drawdown of investing in DJIA every year from the 1st of May to the 31st of October:

Chart 4.3: cumulative return of DJIA from May to October, 1950-2011

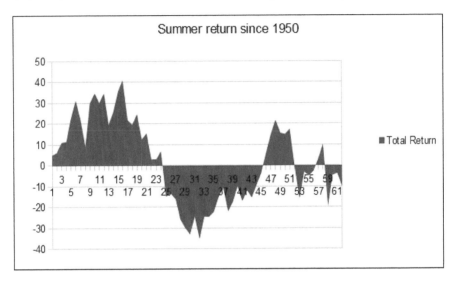

Chart 4.4: cumulative drawdown of DJIA from May to October, 1950-2011

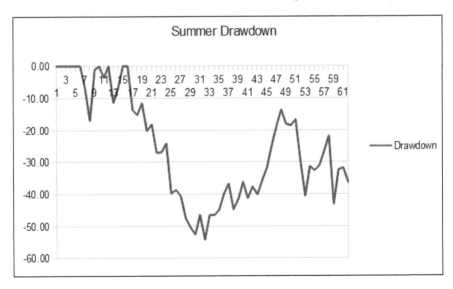

A TWO-SEASON STRATEGY

Jacobsen and Zhang have shown that all countries are not created equal for seasonal patterns. In fact 26 countries out of 108 have an inverted pattern and show a better return in Summer. Here is the list of these countries by region of the world.

- *Europe*: Finland, Cyprus, Bulgaria, Slovenia, Macedonia, Montenegro.

- *South and Central America*: Chile, Peru, El Salvador, Ecuador, Paraguay, Venezuela, Barbados.

- *Africa*: Botswana, Tanzania, Zambia, Mauritius.

- *Asia*: Georgia, Bangladesh, Sri Lanka, Mongolia, Nepal.

- *Middle-East*: Kuwait, Lebanon, Iran, Syria.

To elaborate on our first seasonal strategy, I want to chose one developed and one emerging market. My criteria are the political stability of the country and the region, the availability of an ETF with a sufficient liquidity, and a high average summer gain (according to Jacobsen's publications).

My choices are Singapore and Brazil. Here are the corresponding ETFs:

- EWS: iShares MSCI Singapore Index (inception date March, 11th 1996).

- EWZ: iShares MSCI Brazil Index (inception date July, 9th 2000).

The fact that Brazil is among the most season-sensitive of all stock markets shows that the monthly patterns are similar in the southern hemisphere, although seasons are inverted.

The first version of the strategy is to invest an equal amount in EWS and EWZ 6 months from Nov 1st to Apr 30th, to sell on May 1st and stay in cash until Oct 31st. Gains and dividends of the previous winter are reinvested in an equal weight portfolio every year on the 1st of November.

Here is the chart of the simulation beginning on 8/1/2001 (in red) compared with holding SPY (blue line), with a 0.1% rate for trading costs.

Chart 4.5: investing in EWS and EWZ from November to April

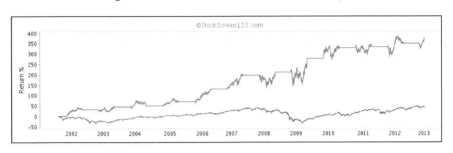

There are losing years starting the 1st of January, but all 12-month periods are winners between two consecutive summers for 11 years. The CAGR is 14.85% and the maximum drawdown -24.32%. The Sortino ratio is 0.48.

To give you an idea of the difference with the U.S. market, here is the chart applying the same seasonal rotation to SPY:

Chart 4.6: investing in SPY from November to April

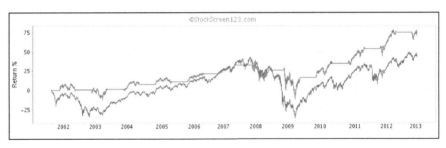

With a CAGR of 5.37% and a drawdown of -33.43%, this is better and less volatile than holding SPY, but far from being as good as the Singapore-Brazil portfolio.

By the way, holding EWS and EWZ for the whole period gives a slightly better average return (16.56%), but an unacceptable drawdown (-63.21%). Just like market timing, the advantage of seasonal strategies is not in increasing the return, but in avoiding the worst drawdowns and lowering the portfolio volatility.

ENHANCING THE PERFORMANCE WITH BONDS

It is possible to increase significantly the return by investing the idle capital in a relatively low-risk asset class during the summer months. It may be bonds, the dollar index or REITs depending on the macroeconomics situation. Here is the result of the simulation investing in EWS and EWZ during the winter, and TLT during the summer (backtest starting on 8/1/2002 to match TLT inception date). The same 0.1% trading rate is used.

Strategy definition: Two-season pattern with Singapore, Brazil and bonds

Name	TwoSeasons-EWS-EWZ
Assets	EWS, EWZ, TLT
Simulation period	8/1/2002-1/1/2013
Re-balanced	1st of May and 1st of November
Positions	1 or 2
Maximum Size	100%
Rules	In TLT from the 1st of May to the 30th of October Equal weight in EWS and EWZ from the 1st of November to the 30th of April
Leverage	1
Transactions costs	0.1%
Benchmark	SPY

Chart 4.7: simulation of TwoSeasons-EWS-EWZ

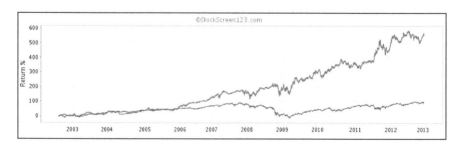

The CAGR is 20.5%, the maximum drawdown -27.1% and the Sortino ratio jumps to 0.89. The values are respectively 13.3%, -24.3% and 0.42 for the version without TLT recalculated on this shorter time interval.

I insist on the fact that the asset choice for the summer depends on the macroeconomics. Long term T-Bonds are not an all-weather shelter. When in doubt, better in cash.

Please note that I never calculate the Kelly criterion for seasonal strategies. This is not laziness: probabilistic gambling theory doesn't make a lot of sense when you play a game only 10 times and once a year.

A FOUR-SEASON STRATEGY

Looking at the seasonality analysis, I came to the following conclusions:

1. January has been the worst month between 1999 and 2012, not only in the U.S.A. Even if it is positive on a longer timeframe, I don't want to be in a game when the odds are against me for at least 14 consecutive years.

2. February has never been a positive month on the long timeframes, and became very negative in the recent period.

3. October is positive on average for at least 50 years, and was the 4th best month of the year between 1999 and 2012, despite the strong fall in October 2008.

So the next idea is to exclude January and February from the good stock season, and to integrate October into it. It leads to a four-season framework:

1. *January and February*: cash, or low-risk asset
2. *March and April*: long stocks
3. *May to September*: cash, or low-risk asset
4. *October to December*: long stocks

Strategy definition: Four-season pattern with various indices and bonds

Name	FourSeasons
Assets	One index ETF and TLT
Simulation period	8/1/2002-1/1/2013
Re-balanced	1st of January, 1st of March, 1st of May and 1st of October Positions 1
Maximum Size	100%
Rules	- TLT from the 1st of January to the 28th or 29th of February - stock index ETF from the 1st of March to the 30th of April - TLT from the 1st of May to the 30th of September - stock index ETF from the 1st of October to the 31st of December
Leverage	1
Transactions costs	0.1%
Benchmark	SPY

I have put the results with different choices of index ETFs for the good seasons in the next table. TLT is taken as the safe asset for the bad seasons.

The table shows the performance of the four-season strategy using SPY, DIA, QQQ and EWG, then the "buy-and-hold" performance for each ETF, and gold (GLD: SPDR Gold Trust).

Table 4.2: Variations of a four-season strategy with different stock index ETFs

8/1/2002-1/1/2013	Total Return	CAGR	DDM	Sortino
FourSeasons with...				
SPY	441.7	17.6	-35.5	0.82
DIA	451.6	17.8	-31.8	0.90
QQQ	586.1	20.3	-35.0	0.96
EWG	1132.0	27.2	-38.4	1.08
Buy & Hold for...				
SPY	98.4	6.8	-55.4	0.17
DIA	98.5	6.8	-51.8	0.18
QQQ	202.6	11.2	-52.4	0.38
EWG	162.3	9.7	-63.9	0.23
TLT	125.7	8.1	-27.0	0.41
Gold (GLD)	437.6	17.6	-30.3	0.81

Some quick conclusions at the first glance:

1. The best return is with EWG: iShares MSCI Germany Index.

2. The best return of U.S. indexes (including small- and mid-cap indexes not shown in the table) is with NASDAQ 100 and its QQQ Powershares ETF.

3. The worst result (with SPY) is "as good as gold" on the period: the return and Sortino ratio are very similar to holding GLD on the same period.

With any choice of equity ETF, not only does the strategy give a higher return than both TLT and the chosen ETF, but the return is higher than *the sum of them*. It means that the strategy did better than holding an equal weight portfolio of both ETFs leveraged twice on margin, without the margin risk. In fact, the drawdown of an equal weight portfolio would be too deep to be held on margin.

Here is the equity curve to help visualizing the EWG/TLT 4-season strategy:

Chart 4.8: Simulation of FourSeasons with EWG as stock index ETF

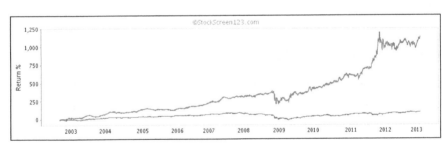

Chart interpretation

The jump during Summer 2011 is due to the surge in T-Bonds: more than +25% in two months. To understand the impact of this exceptional short period, 25% of total return means 2.2% of CAGR over 10 years. Even excluding this interval, the chart and numbers still look good.

The first time I published articles about the 4-season strategies, some readers wrote to me saying T-Bonds may be a bubble (so it would be dangerous in the future) and that most of the strategy performance was due to that (so it would not be representative in the past).

The reality is that in the "EWG-TLT" FourSeasons strategy on this simulation period, the total compound return due to EWG is 471.43% and the return due to TLT is 134.28%. So the seasonal effect on the German stock market is more than 3 times stronger than the interest rates effect in the performance.

When reversing the roles of EWG and TLT for the same period, the EWG return is -57.58% (ouch!) and the TLT return is -11.15%. Even if in a bubble, TLT had a negative average return during the good stock seasons. That shows how powerful the seasonal effects have been, not only on stocks but also on bonds.

However, I understand people who are afraid of T-Bonds in uncertain times.

One way to use the 4-season pattern is to take it as a framework. Consider that you have 2 bags, one for January, February and May to September, and another one for March, April and October to December. Feel free to fill them with tickers and strategies that are consistent with the seasonal effects.

WHY CHOOSE EWG AND NOT ANOTHER COUNTRY ETF?

Jacobsen reports that the German stock market is among the most sensitive to seasons. Before reading his article, I had already noticed that it was one of the most volatile in general.

Chart 4.9: German DAX vs French CAC

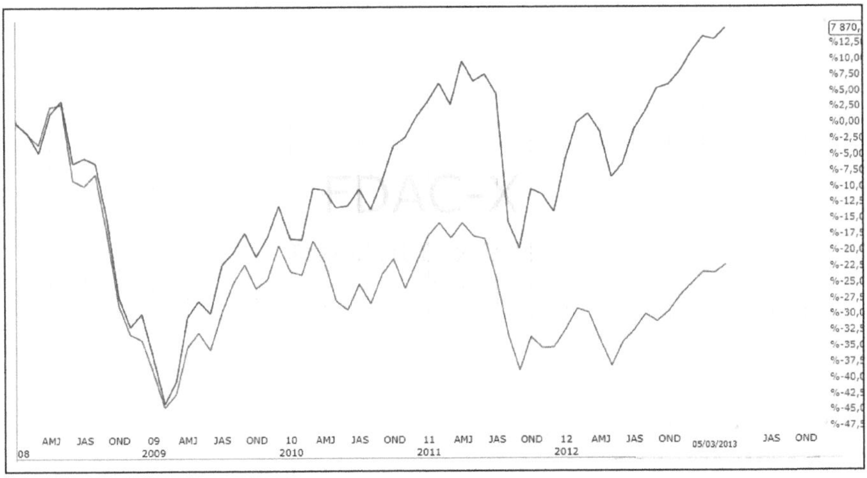

Chart courtesy of freestockcharts.com

This is a 5 year chart of the German DAX index (blue) versus its neighbor the French CAC (brown). Not only is the DAX stronger, but it amplifies the movements in the CAC.

Let's have a look now at the DAX (blue) vs the S&P 500 index (brown) on a shorter time (2 years):

Chart 4.10: DAX vs S&P 500

Chart courtesy of freestockcharts.com

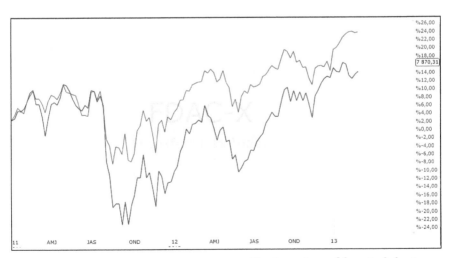

The DAX is weaker now, but an amplification phenomenon is quite obvious again. I had the idea that this amplification would also magnify seasonal effects.

The holdings of EWG are different from the DAX, but it is the simplest way to play the German market as a whole.

Summary of my best 4-season strategy: long TLT in January, February and from May to September, long EWG in April, March and from October to December. This means 2 orders 4 times a year. Time involved: less than 2 minutes per quarter.

THE END OF YEAR PATTERN

The easiest characteristic to explain with seasonals may be why November and December are among the best months of the year. There is a combination of the commercial and psychological impacts of Halloween ("Halloween Effect"), Christmas ("Santa Claus Rally"), accounting optimization, and buying fever driven by fund managers willing to make their portfolios look better at the end of the year ("window dressing").

THE TWO LAST MONTHS

Regardless of the possible reasons (and regardless of the probabilities for the current year), here are the facts: investing in SPY (SPDR S&P 500 ETF) only in November and December from 1/1/1999 to 12/31/2012 would have returned a CAGR of 3% a year (in red on the chart), which is...exactly the same as holding SPY the whole year (in blue).

Chart 4.11: Investing in SPY two months a year in November and December

Indexes, countries and sectors are not created equal for the November-December seasonal pattern. We have seen that the NASDAQ 100 and the German stock markets were good candidates for seasonals.

Here is a table with the returns of investing in QQQ and EWG for just two months a year in November and December for 14 years:

Table 4.3: investing in QQQ and EWG two months a year in November and December

Return w/dividend %	QQQ	EWG
1999	41.3	20.3
2000	-28.5	-0.6
2001	11.8	13.6
2002	-5.0	-4.0
2003	2.4	17.2
2004	9.1	12.4
2005	7.2	12.3
2006	3.7	10.3
2007	-5.7	2.5
2008	-9.1	5.3
2009	13.3	9.8
2010	4.6	0.3
2011	-0.1	-2.8
2012	1.9	5.8
Average	3.4	7.3

In both cases, investing in the index for only 2 months of the year did much better than holding it all the year from 1/1/1999 to 1/1/2013 (CAGR: 2.4% for QQQ and 3.1% for EWG). The result is especially impressive for the German index.

DECEMBER

Let's focus on the month of December, which is relatively even stronger. It was positive for the S&P index 11 times out of 14 between 1999 and 2012. I have shown in an article published on Seeking Alpha that there was a strong rally in small caps between the beginning of the month and Christmas, and another one in the technology big caps the last days of the months. Two industries are especially affected by this last "window dressing" rally: internet software & services, and communication equipments.

SEASONS AND SECTORS

It may be dangerous to look for seasonal patterns in sector ETFs. Indeed the superposition of cycles of different and variable lengths make things much more complicated. That's why in the seasonal area I have a strong preference for strategies on general indexes.

Three sectors have had regularly strong months in Winter during the last decade: Energy, Utilities and Telecommunications.

I have also noted that between 2001 and 2012, Real Estate and REITs were the only sectors to perform relatively well in bad seasons.

I would like to report a strategy about sectors. It exploits the winter patterns of Energy and Utilities sectors and has a three-season pattern:

- *January to April*: Energy (IYE)
- *October to December*: Utilities (IDU)
- *Rest of the time*: T-Bonds (TLT)

Strategy definition: Three-season pattern with Energy, Utilities and Bonds

Name	ThreeSeasons-Sectors
Assets	IYE, IDU, TLT
Simulation period	8/1/2002-1/1/2013
Re-balanced	1st of January, 1st of May and 1st of October
Positions	1
Maximum Size	100%
Rules	IYE from the 1st of January to the 30th of April TLT from the 1st of May to the 30th of September IDU from the 1st of October to the 31st of December
Leverage	1
Transactions costs	0.1%
Benchmark	SPY

This gives the following results on the same period:

- CAGR: 19.2%

- Max Drawdown: -33.4%

- Sortino ratio: 0.77

As a conclusion about seasonals and sectors, the trial confirms the theory of cycles: it is difficult to find a profitable specific seasonal pattern with sectors. Seasonal patterns give better results with global indexes. It is possible to find something in industries and sub-industries, but then ETFs, when they exist, are too illiquid or too recent to be seriously backtested. They are thus out of the scope of this book.

MORE SEASONAL PATTERNS

After the previous sections, if you are not convinced that seasonal patterns should not be ignored in your plan, you will never be! In fact, seasonals are everywhere. Not only in stock indexes and bonds, but also in currencies, precious metals and commodities.

The next table summarizes the historical monthly trends for the price of futures contracts for 40 years. For every month and every asset, a number represents the magnitude of the trend. For example, 1 means than the monthly average return is roughly between 1% and 2%; -3 means that it is between -3% and -4%. An empty cell means no significant trend (between -1% and 1% on average).

The "year" column gives the number of years in historical data, which is not the same for all assets.

The "ETF" column gives the most liquid ETF or ETN for each asset. Remember that the trends have been calculated on the futures and not on the funds whose start dates are more recent.

The "Swing" column gives the sum of monthly magnitude in absolute values for each asset. You can interpret it as the very roughly approximate return of an hypothetical swing trade, being long the good months and short the bad ones.

Table 4.4: monthly trends for some assets

Asset	Years	ETF	Swing	Jan	Feb	Mar	Apr	May	Jun	Jul	Aug	Sep	Oct	Nov	Dec
DJIA	40	DIA	7			1	2					-1		1	2
Nasdaq	36	QQQ	7	3								-1		1.5	1.5
DAX	16	EWG	15	-2	-5	3	3	2							
Euro	35	FXE	3.5	-1.5								1			1
Gold	40	GLD	9	1	1			1.5				2.5		1.5	1.5
Silver	37	SLV	13.5	2	1				-2	2.5		3.5	-1		1.5
Platinum	32	PPLT	9	2	1	-1		2	-1	1			1		
Palladium	30	PALL	7.5	5.5				-1	-1						
Copper	37	JJC	13		2	3		-2	-1	2		2	1		
Oil	24	OIL, USO	18.5			3	3	1.5		4	3	-2	-2		
NatGas	17	UNG	21	-4		4			-3	-2		-5	-3		
Sugar	37	SGG	14.5	1	-2	-3				-3	-1	3	1.5		
Coffee	37	JO	7						-5						2
Cocoa	37	NIB	7.5						2.5	2		-3			

The data are measured and calculated from the charts by Dimitri Speck available on seasonalcharts.com.

You may draw as many conclusions and hypotheses as you wish from this table; I will just focus on what appears the most important to me:

1. There is a bullish seasonal trend on metals from November to February.

2. Gold has had no calendar month below -1% on average for 40 years.

3. Sugar and coffee have been in a long term bearish trend for 37 years, and Cocoa in a bullish trend.

The highest historical probability of being whipsawed is in platinum, silver and copper.

I would like to mention four important warnings:

1. It is not a strategy description: the moves against the historical trend may be strong in commodities. Without speaking of the currency war disturbing the historical cycles.

2. The numbers do not have the probabilistic value of a backtest: the data availability period is different from one asset to another.

3. Check the contango on futures before taking any position in a commodity ETF or ETN. (If you don't know what contango is, learn it or avoid commodities.)

4. ETNs have a higher counterparty risk than future contracts.

These historical facts should not be used as the base of a strategy, but they can be used as a filter or a confirmation to improve one's timing. For example, it is probably better to avoid being short on palladium in January, or long coffee in June, except when all other indicators strongly confirm the trade. On the other hand, a weak technical buy signal on palladium in January would be reinforced in the light of seasonal trends.

CHAPTER SUMMARY

- Recent academic research shows that seasonal patterns are as old as stock markets and have been even stronger in recent decades.

- Two seasonal models based on two and four seasons are proposed.

- Performance may be enhanced by investing in bond ETFs during the bad season for stocks.

- All indices and all countries are not equal for seasonals. Some of the best performing strategies during the last decade use country ETFs on Germany, Brazil and Singapore.

- The end-of-year rally is especially strong for technological and German stocks.

- Looking for seasonal patterns among big sectors is difficult, however a three-season model is proposed using energy, utilities and bonds.

- Finally some seasonal patterns are listed in commodities.

CHAPTER 5:

MIXING STRATEGIES

THIS CHAPTER EXPLORES TWO WAYS OF MIXING anomalies to reduce risk: mixing the rules to create a new strategy, and investing separately in them with money management rules. Various blends of previous strategies are proposed and simulated. The chapter ends with a discussion about probabilities, luck and their impact on one's portfolio.

AN ATTEMPT TO COMBINE EVERYTHING

When identifying valuable anomalies, there is an irrepressible temptation to try to mix them.

The Top 6 sectors strategy seen previously already combines four patterns:

1. A global market timing rule

2. An individual timing rule

3. A momentum ranking rule

4. Moreover the version including IEF integrates the hypothesis of negative correlation between stocks and bonds.

What about adding a seasonal rule?

It can be done in two ways:

1. *Agressive approach*: use "AND" combination of conditions to exit equities. That is to say that the protective mode is activated only if it is a bad month and the market timing is bad.

2. *Defensive approach*: use "OR" combination of conditions to exit equities. That is to say, the portfolio is systematically in protective mode on the bad months. Market timing and momentum rules are applied on the good ones.

The following table shows the simulation results on the Top 6 sectors. The conditions are the same as in the original *Sectors-Top6-IEF* strategy seen before: weekly checking and rebalancing, 0.1% trading costs and a 2% borrowing rate when leveraged. The protective mode is 100% in IEF.

Table 5.1: variations of the strategy Sectors-Top6-IEF combined with seasonal rules

8/1/2002-1/1/2013	Total Return	CAGR	DDM	Sortino	Kelly	Sterling	DD-lengthMax
SPY Buy & Hold	98.8	6.8	-55.4	0.39			
Sectors-Top6-IEF	234.9	12.3	-16.2	0.79	0.17	0.47	62 weeks
Agressive	141.7	8.8	-18.7	0.39	0.13	0.31	94 weeks
Defensive	164.6	9.8	-11.2	0.75	0.19	0.46	64 weeks
Defensive leveraged x2	486.9	17.7	-22.8	0.88	0.17	0.54	112 weeks

Both aggressive and defensive seasonal rule additions are pretty bad for the returns. However, the defensive version cuts the drawdown by nearly one third and makes the strategy eligible for leveraging. Then the Sortino ratio jumps to 0.88. The drawback is that the drawdown maximum length also jumps from 14 months to 25 months (probably due to borrowing rate and a long flat period on the non-leveraged strategy).

Finally, regarding all factors and the intrinsic risk of leveraging, the original "Top 6 / IEF" strategy may stay the best one.

THE "NO BRAIN NO GAIN" STRATEGY

That's the name I gave to one of the simplest and safest aggregate strategies. It uses only three ETFs and two different trading rules.

The first strategy is a 4-season strategy with QQQ (NASDAQ 100 ETF) and TLT.

The second one is the MDY/TLT paired switching.

I summarize:

- *Position 1*: TLT in January and February and from May to September, QQQ in March and April and from October to December.
- *Position 2*: choose between MDY and TLT the highest 60-day return.

The position size is limited to 50% of the portfolio.

Strategy definition: Mixing a four-season pattern and paired switching

Name	NoBrainNoGain
Assets	QQQ, MDY, TLT
Simulation period	1/1/2003-1/1/2013
Re-balanced	Weekly
Positions	2
Maximum Size	50%
Rules	Position 1: defined by FourSeasons-QQQ Position 2: defined by PairedSwitching-Index-TLT (with Index ETF = MDY)
Leverage	1
Transactions costs	0.1%
Benchmark	SPY

Here are the results from 1/1/2003 to 1/1/2013, with 0.1% fees and a weekly rebalancing:

- CAGR: 16%
- Maximum Drawdown: -13%
- Sortino Ratio: 1.27

Chart 5.1: simulation of the strategy NoBrainNoGain

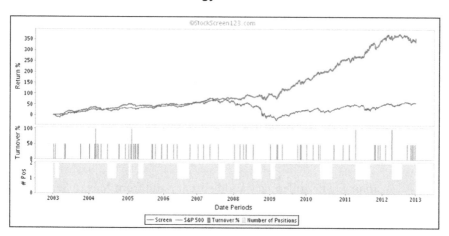

Why is this combination working well?

The seasonal strategy can be considered as the foundation. When seasons are consistent with the statistics, the paired-switching follows the same trend, else it acts as a hedge.

BUILDING A SYSTEMIC PORTFOLIO

Combining the rules of two good strategies doesn't always make a winner. Quantitative analysis is about modeling complex systems: companies, groups of investors, and their interactions. The first characteristic, and definition, of a complex system, is that its behavior is not the result of compounding its parts' behaviors. You may combine two winning models, and get something worse than the originals.

That is why it is often better to bet separately on reasonably good strategies using money management rules, than to try to mix them. Don't take this as a definitive rule: we have already seen that mixing market timing and momentum could improve both the return and the drawdown.

Systemic complexity is also why every little change in a quantitative model must be followed by new simulations and their interpretation. The examples I will show now are also representative of my vision of diversification. In my opinion, it is much better to diversify a portfolio with 3 or 4 ETF strategies relying on distinct anomalies, regardless of the number of positions, than to hold 20 stocks or more.

I propose to combine 3 reasonable unleveraged strategies we have seen up to now:

1. The momentum "top 5" tactical allocation on global assets

2. The seasonal on Singapore and Brazil (2 seasons)

3. The seasonal on Germany (4 seasons)

To simplify the portfolio management, the rebalancing is performed once a week at the same time for all strategies. It means that the seasonal rotation may not occur right on the 1st of a month and may be delayed up to 6 days.

I use the following rules to build the compound portfolio:

- all selected tickers are equal weight.

- when a ticker is selected more than one time (it may be the case for the bond ETF), it counts as only one position.

Doing so, the portfolio has a maximum of 8 positions: 5 on tactical allocation, 3 on seasonals. The next table gives the simulation results compared with the three individual strategies.

MONEY MANAGEMENT

Two money management variants are tested: with a position limit of 12.5% (1/8), and with a position limit of 25%. As the first one has a relatively low drawdown, the leveraged version is also presented. The same rates as before are applied: 0.1% for trading and 2% for borrowing the leveraged part.

Table 5.2: results of three previous strategies and their various combinations

6/1/2003-1/1/2013	Total Return	CAGR	DDM	Sortino	Kelly	Sterling	DD-lengthMax
individual strategies							
Assets-Top5	277.1	14.9	-13.7	0.96	0.20	0.63	88 weeks
TwoSeasons-EWS-EWZ	402.7	18.3	-27.1	0.76	0.16	0.49	49 weeks
FourSeasons with EWG	674.5	23.8	-32.3	0.94	0.22	0.56	62 weeks
combining the 3 strategies							
limited size12.5%	298.8	15.5	-12.5	1.11	0.22	0.67	87 weeks
limited size 12.5% lev. x2	1146.2	30.1	-24.5	1.23	0.22	0.87	88 weeks
limited size 25%	424.1	18.9	-19.6	1.19	0.21	0.64	46 weeks

Here is the equity curve of the leveraged version:

Chart 5.2: simulation of the combination with a 12.5% position size limit and leveraged twice

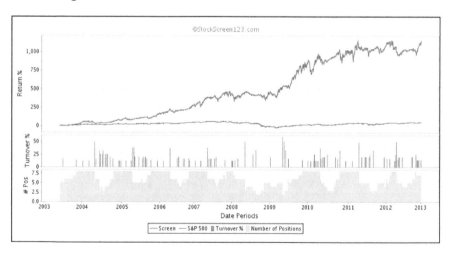

The simulation statistical report shows that, on average, six positions out of eight are filled and one changes every 3 weeks.

It needs a weekly checking, but most of the time there is nothing to do.

WEIGHT VECTORS

It may be also interesting to test different weights for each strategy. In the following table, each line represents a portfolio distribution between the three strategies.

For example (5,2,1) means: $\frac{5}{8}$ of the portfolio in global assets, $\frac{2}{8}$ in the 2 seasons model, $\frac{1}{8}$ in the 4 seasons model. Although it looks the same as above, you will note that the results differ a little bit. Testing different weight vectors is easier when applying money management rules separately on each strategy. The differences with the previous combined versions are that:

- The bond ETF position may be duplicated if it is selected in two strategies,

- The position limit applies separately on strategies.

Table 5.3: results of various weighted combinations of the same three strategies

6/1/2003-1/1/2013	CAGR	DDM	Kelly	Sterling	DD-lengthMax
5,2,1	17.6	-12.1	0.24	0.80	39 weeks
5,0,2	18.0	-11.6	0.24	0.83	59 weeks
5,2,0	16.6	-13.3	0.22	0.71	41 weeks
1,0,1	20.1	-16.5	0.26	0.76	62 weeks

Among the four tested options, it appears that the best return and the lowest drawdown are achieved without the Singapore-Brazil strategy, respectively with (1,0,1) and (5,0,2) as weight vectors.

The shortest maximum drawdown duration is achieved including the Singapore-Brazil strategy. In fact there is not a "best" weight vector. Each strategy works with the others to enhance a particular quality. The first one brings a moderate but steady return with a low risk, the second one shortens the maximum duration in drawdown, the third one brings an additional return.

As a consequence, investors with various risk profiles and various horizons may make different choices.

THE LUCK FACTOR

Even if the numbers look great, you must never forget the underlying hypotheses of the models.

The Sortino ratio makes sense with a Gaussian statistical distribution of the return, the Kelly criterion with a constant probability and gain/loss ratio, and the maximum drawdown makes sense if the simulation period has covered market conditions bad enough.

To give an example of the influence of a small variation in the model, let's take the example of compounding the strategies with a (5,2,1) weight vector.

- The dataset has 501 weekly returns
- The average gain/average loss ratio is 1.02
- The experimental probability of a winning week is 61.6%

Taking into account the dataset size, the probability with a 95% confidence interval is 57.2%. It means that I have measured a probability of 61.6% on a set of 501 data, but in fact the real probability of the game may be higher or lower. In this case a formula of statistics tells us that the real probability has a 95% chance to be higher than 57.2%.

Is this difference so important?

In this case, it remains a winning game, but the Kelly criterion falls from 0.24 to 0.16. Drawing 100 random equity curves based on probabilities looks like this:

Chart 5.3: beams of possible equity curves depending on the probability of winning game, for a fixed average win/average loss ratio

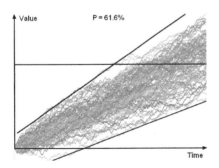
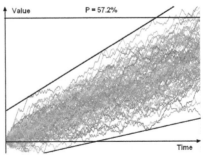

The horizontal line represents the same objective on both charts.

The best case scenario to reach the objective is significantly longer in the second one, and the uncertainty is also higher. Losing periods and bad luck have a stronger influence on the long term when there is a small variation or unappreciation of the probability.

When for any reason a strategy is over-rated (methodology, insufficient sample of data and market conditions, etc.), the beam representing possible futures for the portfolio value may be wider, than you think. The wider the beam, the less certain the profitability. Using anomalies confirmed by academic research and testing them on a decade gives us an edge, not a guarantee.

CHAPTER SUMMARY

- The best way to mix good strategies is not to create a new one mixing the rules, but to invest in them separately using money management rules.

- Investing in strategies based on different logics systematically lowers the drawdown and may improve the risk-adjusted performance ratios.

- The easiest way to experiment with this idea is to mix a seasonal strategy and a paired-switching strategy: I called this concept No Brain No Gain.

- Other examples are given using momentum and seasonal strategies from the previous chapters.

- Different money management options are exposed, including position size limitation, weight vectors, and leveraging. However risk-based position sizing is not covered in this book.

- The conclusion shows the danger of overrating the quality ratios and gives an idea of what is really "luck".

CHAPTER 6:

FUNDAMENTAL QUANTITATIVE MODELS

THIS CHAPTER IS A QUICK INTRODUCTION to quantitative fundamental analysis. The focus is on keeping things simple and practical with common tools for individual investors. It begins with hypotheses, then presents three models, each one oriented towards a category of fundamental data. It also compares market timing and hedging to protect a portfolio in specific cases. It ends with an example of a low-risk portfolio mixing the three models.

HYPOTHESES

Existing publications by or about famous investors like Graham, Buffett, Zweig, Greenblatt, Piotroski and O'Neil extensively cover the topic of quantitative fundamental analysis. I won't go into the details here and suggest you refer to these publications if you want to learn more about fundamental analysis. It seems that each model's efficiency varies over time, depending on market conditions and other factors.

Investors should never forget that institutions make the prices. What is important is not if a model is accurate in telling what a stock is worth, but if it is accurate to follow or anticipate the moves of institutional money.

My aim here is to give you three directions to explore, based on the three concepts that motivate investors and institutions for buying a stock:

1. value,

2. growth,

3. dividend.

The models presented here share some intentional limitations to make them actionable as simply as possible by individual investors, including:

- The universe is big-cap only: S&P 500 companies

- The set of indicators and rules is kept very small

- The rules can be implemented in free or low-cost screeners

- No formula, variables or complicated rules are used

- Simulations show that these models have been reasonably profitable in the last decade. Feel free to take them as is or to tweak them to improve them.

A VALUE MODEL

This model uses three valuation ratios, comparing the stock price to book value, cash flow and earnings.

FILTER RULES

- S&P 500 companies only

- Price-to-book ratio (last quarter) < 8

- Price-to-cash flow per share ratio (TTM) < 10

- Price Earnings Ratio, excluding extraordinary items (TTM) < 20

- Average analyst recommendation <=3 (hold or better)

RANKING RULE

Sort pre-selected companies by increasing Total Debt to Equity ratio (lower is better).

MARKET TIMING RULE

Sell all stocks if S&P500 index current year EPS estimate falls below its value 15 weeks ago. Buy the selected stocks again if it is strictly above.

Checking/Rebalancing: every 4 weeks.

REMARKS

The filter is not very restrictive. At the time of writing about 25% of the S&P 500 companies pass the test.

Here are the results of 14-year simulations taking the top N companies, for N=20, N=10 and N=6. With a lower number of stocks, the return goes down and the drawdown goes up. In most strategies I have tested, having 4 to 8 positions is often a sweet spot offering a good compromise of return and volatility. The simulations take into account a 0.2% rate (spread and trading fee).

Table 6.1: variations of a value oriented strategy with the position number

1/1/1999-1/1/2013	Total Return	CAGR	DDM	Sortino
SPY Buy & Hold	50.6	3.0	-55.4	-0.07
Top 20	393.3	12.1	-32.8	0.52
Top 10	526.0	14.0	-33.2	0.63
Top 6	573.2	14.6	-28.5	0.64

Name	Value-Top6
Assets	S&P 500 stocks
Simulation period	1/1/1999-1/1/2013
Re-balanced	4-Week
Positions	6
Maximum Size	16.7%
Market Timing	S&P500 current year EPS estimate above or equals to its value 15 weeks ago
Filters	S&P 500 members Price-to-book ratio (last quarter) < 8 Price-to-cash flow per share ratio (TTM) < 10 Price Earnings Ratio, excluding extraordinary items (TTM) < 20 Average analyst recommendation <=3 (hold or better)
Selection	The 6 stocks with the lowest Total Debt to Equity ratio (ranking rule)
Leverage	1
Transactions costs	0.2%
Benchmark	SPY

Here is the chart to visualize the Top 6 selection:

Chart 6.1: simulation of the "Value-Top6" strategy

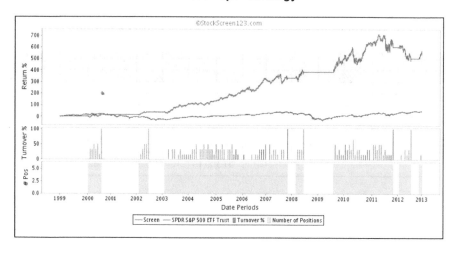

The average turnover per rebalancing is 19%. It means that there is about 1 position change on average every 4 weeks.

A GROWTH MODEL

In this model growth must be confirmed on two levels: sales and earning per share.

FILTER RULES

- S&P 500 companies only
- EPS percent change, last quarter vs. previous quarter > 5%
- Sales percent change, last quarter vs. same quarter of previous year > 5%
- Price-to-cash flow per share ratio (quarterly) < 8
- Relative Strength Index: RSI(14) < 70

RANKING RULE

Same as before-

- Sort pre-selected companies by increasing Total Debt to Equity ratio (lower is better).

MARKET TIMING RULE

Same as before-

- Sell portfolio if S&P500 Current Year EPS Estimate falls below its value 15 weeks ago. Buy again if it is strictly above.
- Checking/Rebalancing (same as before): every 4 weeks.

The filtering rules are not 100% growth based: they include one rule on valuation (price to cash flow) and a rule to avoid overbought stocks from a technical point of view (RSI below 70).

The filter is much more restrictive than for the previous model: for example, at the time of writing only 18 stocks pass the test. The following table shows simulation results for the Top N companies, for N=10, N=6 and N=4. The trading fee rate is the same as before and I add a money management rule: the individual position size is limited to 1/N of the portfolio.

Table 6.2: variations of a growth oriented strategy with the position number

1/1/1999-1/1/2013	Total Return	CAGR	DDM	Sortino
SPY Buy & Hold	50.6	3.0	-55.4	-0.07
Top 10	479.9	13.3	-29.1	0.54
Top 6	628.5	15.2	-26.6	0.64
Top 4	1197.0	20.0	-25.3	0.92

Strategy definition: Top 4 stocks for the specified Growth model

Name	Growth-Top4
Assets	S&P 500 stocks
Simulation period	1/1/1999-1/1/2013
Re-balanced	4-Week
Positions	4
Maximum Size	25%
Market Timing	S&P500 current year EPS estimate above or equal to its value 15 weeks ago
Filters	S&P 500 members EPS percent change, last quarter vs. previous quarter > 5% Sales percent change, last quarter vs same quarter last year > 5% Price-to-cash flow per share ratio (quarterly) < 8 Relative Strength Index: RSI(14) < 70
Selection	The 4 stocks with the lowest Total Debt to Equity ratio
Leverage	1
Transactions costs	0.2%
Benchmark	SPY

Chart 6.2: simulation of the "Growth-Top4" strategy

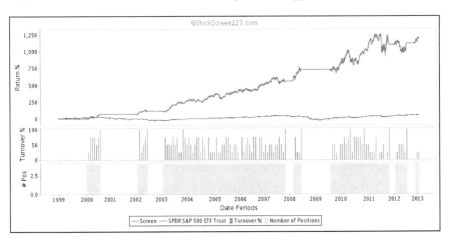

The average turnover per rebalancing is 33%. One third of the portfolio on average (1.33 positions) is renewed every 4 weeks.

A DIVIDEND MODEL

This model focuses on stocks whose dividend yield is above 4%, both for the latest value and the 5-year average.

FILTER RULES

- S&P 500 companies only
- Average Dividend Yield last 5 years > 4%
- Current Dividend Yield > 4%
- Short Interest / Float < 5%
- Utilities sector is excluded

RANKING RULE

Same as before:

- Sort pre-selected companies by increasing Total Debt to Equity ratio (lower is better).

MARKET TIMING RULE

Same as before:

- Sell portfolio if S&P500 Current Year EPS Estimate falls below its value 15 weeks ago. Buy again if it is strictly above.
- Checking/Rebalancing (same as before): every 4 weeks.

Filter rules are very restrictive: at the time of writing only 12 companies are selected. It would be 26 including Utilities. This sector has been excluded to avoid an excessive concentration in one sector. Utilities also statistically lower significantly the performance of this model. This model works better when diversified: keeping the Top 10 stocks with a position size limited to 10% gives good results.

Strategy definition: Top 10 stocks for the specified Dividend model

Name	Dividend-Top10
Assets	S&P 500 stocks
Simulation period	1/1/1999-1/1/2013 Re-balanced 4-Week
Positions	10
Maximum Size	10%
Market Timing	S&P500 current year EPS estimate above or equal to its value 15 weeks ago
Filters	S&P 500 members Utilities sector excluded Average Dividend Yield last 5 years > 4% Current Dividend Yield > 4% Short Interest / Float < 5%
Selection	The 10 stocks with the lowest Total Debt to Equity ratio
Leverage	1
Transactions costs	0.2%
Benchmark	SPY

Because of data availability, the simulation starts in 2001. For comparison purposes, the SPY benchmark and the two previous strategies have been re-simulated on 12 years.

Table 6.3: variations of a value oriented strategy with the position number

1/1/2001-1/1/2013	Total Return	CAGR	DDM	Sortino
SPY Buy & Hold	43.3	3.0	-55.4	-0.04
Value-Top6	489.0	15.9	-28.5	0.74
Growth-Top4	665.4	18.5	-25.3	0.86
Dividend-Top10	400.7	14.3	-17.3	0.89

The dividend strategy has the lowest (but decent) return, the best drawdown and the highest Sortino ratio.

Chart 6.3: simulation of the Dividend strategy

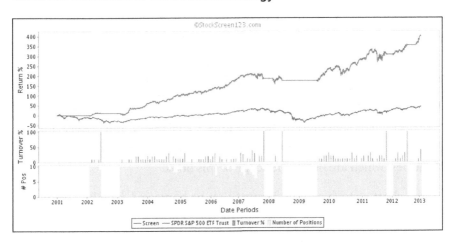

The average turnover per rebalancing is 12% (1.2 position).

MARKET TIMING AND HEDGING

THE CONTRIBUTION OF MARKET TIMING

If we drop the market timing rule, the average returns are still decent. They stay for the three strategies in a 12%-17% range. But the drawdown jumps to unacceptable levels: 55 to 65%.

As we have already seen for indexes, the main benefit of market timing is not in increasing the return but in limiting the volatility and drastically cutting the drawdowns. As for ETF strategies, you can also invest in T-Bonds when the portfolio is out of equities.

WHAT ABOUT HEDGING?

There are basically two techniques to protect a position: going out of it fully or partially when an indicator tells us (this is market timing), or holding an inverse position in a correlated, underperforming asset (this is hedging).

For the Value-Growth-Dividend trilogy, I have introduced a market timing rule without justification. I would like to explain my choice now. The three strategies have been simulated in three versions: normal (N), hedged (H) and with the market timing rule using the S&P 500 EPS estimate (T).

The simulated hedging tactic is as simple as possible: an amount equal to the long positions is sold short in the benchmark ETF (SPY). You can also imagine buying an inverse ETF (SH for example). Sophisticated investors prefer option strategies, which are out of the scope of this book.

To sell short a stock or ETF, it must first be borrowed. The borrowing rate may be different from one broker to another. I take 2% here.

When using an inverse ETF, buying it on margin would cost more or less the same rate.

Table 6.4: variations of the three strategies (N: normal, H: hedged, T: timed)

1/1/2001-1/1/2013	Total Return	CAGR	DDM	Sortino
Value-Top6-N	510.2	16.3	-57.0	0.52
Value-Top6-H	287.0	11.9	-27.1	0.66
Value-Top6-T	489.0	15.9	-28.5	0.74
Growth-Top4-N	371.2	13.8	-64.0	0.40
Growth-Top4-H	182.9	9.1	-35.5	0.34
Growth-Top4-T	665.4	18.5	-25.3	0.86
Dividend-Top10-N	313.6	12.5	-59.2	0.46
Dividend-Top10-H	110.5	6.4	-28.0	0.29
Dividend-Top10-T	400.7	14.3	-17.3	0.89

First remark: the normal Value strategy has a higher return than both protected versions, however the difference is not significant with the market-timed one. On the other hand, both protected versions divide the original drawdown by two.

For the three strategies, market timing gives a better return and a higher Sortino ratio than hedging. The maximum drawdowns are also better, or similar in the case of the Value strategy.

COMBINING MODELS

The Dividend strategy is the safest one, regarding both the volatility and the return variability with the starting date.

The idea here is to build a conservative portfolio allocating 50% of the capital to the Dividend-Top10 strategy, 25% to the Value-Top6 and 25% to the Growth-Top4.

The positions are equal weight inside each strategy. Doing so, a dividend position is worth 5% of the total, a value position 4.17% and a growth position 6.25%.

The simulation is done from 1/1/2001 to 1/1/2013.

Here are the numbers:

Average Return/4-week period (%)	**1.2**
CAGR (%)	16
Maximum Drawdown (%)	-10.4
Drawdown Max. Duration (months)	19
Sterling ratio	0.78
Kelly ratio	0.54
Kelly ratio (using probability with a 95% confidence interval)	0.4

The mix brings two unexpected good surprises: a very robust Kelly ratio and a low drawdown. More aggressive investors might find here a possible candidate for leveraging.

A cautionary note however: here the drawdown is calculated at the end of 4-week periods, not in real time. It may be significantly worse on daily close and cannot be compared with previous values of individual strategies simulations. Moreover the past drawdowns are not very deep but some of them are long.

CHAPTER SUMMARY

- Three simple fundamental quantitative models for the S&P 500 universe are presented.

- Each of them is based on a category of fundamental ratios: valuation ratios, growth ratios, and dividend yields.

- Market timing is an important component of the models, and gives better results than hedging in this case.

- A weighted combination of three models is proposed as a low-risk dynamic stock portfolio.

CHAPTER 7:

DESIGNING A STRATEGY

THIS BOOK CONTAINS STRATEGIES that can be implemented as they are described. It can also be considered by advanced readers as a starting point to design their own rules and portfolios. The key point of the process is backtesting, which is known to be a dangerous endeavour. It would be irresponsible to show the way to the jungle without giving some basic advice and a list of pitfalls to avoid. This is the aim of this last chapter.

THE FRAMEWORK

Choosing a trading style

The most important factor when designing strategies is to know the trading style you want to work with. It depends on your psychology, your available time, your lifestyle. Depending on your situation, you may want to trade only once a month, or are available to trade once a day or intraday. The strategies described in this book are designed for people who want to trade once a week or once a month. This is compatible with most professional and personal situations. Trading schedules can be planned on fixed days at fixed hours, independently of how the market is moving. There is no need for real-time or even daily monitoring, and no need for a high-speed internet connection.

You have also to choose the types of instruments you will be trading.

This book is limited to liquid stocks and ETFs, excluding leveraged products. They are the easiest to backtest and the safest to trade. Trading leveraged products requires more skill and close monitoring.

The trading style is *your* choice. A very active and skilled investor can work on different timescales with different types of instruments. However it is very unlikely to have success in a trading style that doesn't match your knowledge, personality and lifestyle. This is a reason why 95% of forex and CFD retail traders lose money.

Start from a documented bias anomaly

All investment methods, and by extension all trading systems, are based on one or more anomalies. Most of them, if not all, fall into one of the following four categories:

1. **Reversal**: fundamental (valuation) or technical (divergence, patterns)

2. **Continuation**: fundamental (growth) or technical (momentum, patterns)

3. **Habits**: timed patterns and reactions to planned events

4. **Rhythm**: there are likely and unlikely behaviors on a given timescale; for example, a three-month rally will not consolidate in minutes

Unless you are yourself working in financial research, it's better to start from professional and academic publications, adapt ideas to your trading style, and maybe improve them. Research papers often stay at a general level and disclose only a part of the benefit you can draw from an anomaly.

There are online libraries of academic publications in finance, like the Social Science Research Network Library. A drawback is that they are so large that you must already have an idea of what you are looking for. Another problem is that authors often use complicated mathematical language.

Choosing your tools

You need tools for three stages of a strategy life cycle:

- design,
- implementation,
- control.

1. DESIGN

Designing a strategy is an iterative process including research, translation in logical rules, simulation, evaluation and validation.

Fig 7.1: Designing a strategy is an iterative process

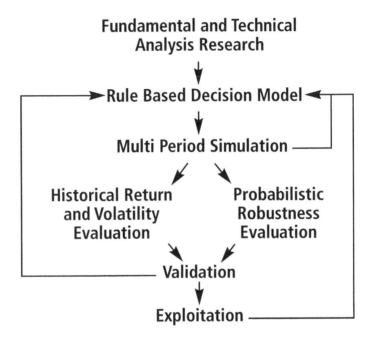

For the design, you have to simulate and evaluate strategies. If they are simple, downloading historical price series from any free data source and putting them into your own spreadsheets is a good way to start.

When things become more complicated, backtesting features are integrated into trading software such as MetaTrader and NinjaTrader. The drawback is that they are limited to technical strategies and it is necessary to learn a procedural programming language. The best choice for an individual investor is to buy software or subscribe to a simulation platform with a professional and daily updated database.

Online platforms and specific software offer the possibility to build strategies with a rule-based language. The best services will naturally change over time, look for the keywords *screener backtest stock ETF,* in your search engine. As I write this, three or four decent simulation service providers are appearing on the first page of search results. To write this book and to design most of my strategies I have used Portfolio123 (see the appendix).

2. IMPLEMENTATION

For the implementation you need a screener (generally the same platform you use for simulations, but that is not an obligation), and a low-cost broker. If you want to automate your trades, programmable trading software and programming skills are needed.

3. CONTROL

For the control, simple spreadsheets are suitable to track your trades and compare them to a post-simulation.

THE DEADLY SINS OF BACKTESTING

Backtesting is a dangerous exercise. This chapter presents a non-exhaustive list of pitfalls.

Forgetting time factors

A simulation should use only data that were available at every decision point in the past. Make sure that your database has no bias by design:

- It must contain disappeared companies (or else your model suffers from survivor bias).

- Index-based universes must be timestamped (the S&P 500 list is not the same today and 10 years ago).

- The fundamental data must be correctly timestamped and available at the specified date. Sometimes it's good to verify if the current portfolio given in your screener has not changed in the simulation at the same date some days or weeks later...

Make also sure that your own methodology has no look-ahead bias:

- Defining a simulation universe from a current list of winners or from a current dividend aristocrats list is a methodological mistake.

- When using moving averages, make sure that the average stops on the day before the decision point, not on the same day. This kind of mistake may be hidden and fatal when designing your own spreadsheets.

In the series of time-related problems, beware of embedded stop-loss and take-profit orders in your strategies. The simulation engine takes the OHLC data (prices on Open, High, Low, Close) and makes a guess on the route between the two fixed points: Open and Close. The only thing we know is that the hypothesis is not the reality. If the Low/High interval is broader than the stop-loss/take-profit interval, the simulation can decide to trigger the take-profit first, when it was the stop-loss in the real world.

Your simulation might transform real gains to losses...or the reverse. If you add a limit-buy order, the simulation can even show a gain or a loss on a position that is still open in reality.

Forgetting liquidity

When you begin to become familiar with your simulation tool, you may find unbelievable things. The kind of strategies that should make you a billionaire in less than 10 years. The problem (unless you are a genius) is that they are absolutely unrealistic. Most of the time, illiquid stocks and penny stocks are included by default in the simulation universe.

There are two problems with these companies:

1. The volume of transactions may not be sufficient to build a sizeable position.

2. Even if it is, the bid/ask spread and the volumes available in the order book will lead to a real price which may be worse by 5%, 10% or more than the theoretical simulated price.

In the marvelous world of small and micro caps, there is no guarantee that a stock is available for trading at the displayed bid/ask prices. More often than you wish an order with an insignificant volume hides a much farther real price.

You can limit or eliminate the liquidity risk by filtering companies:

- on a minimum daily average volume (in shares or in value),

- on a minimum market capital,

- on a predefined universe based on indexes (S&P 500, NASDAQ 100 for example).

Forgetting trading costs

Even with a low-cost broker, trading fees can have a heavy drag, especially on intraday and daily strategies. Two charts will show it better than a long chapter.

You may have heard of a strategy called "4-2", supposed to be profitable. It consists of buying stocks that have gone down four consecutive days, and selling them two days later. Here are the simulation charts on the Dow Jones Industrial Average companies for 14 years, first forgetting trading costs, then with $10 fee for $10,000 invested (0.1%). Trades are made on open.

With trading costs = 0:

Chart 7.1: simulation of the "4-2" strategy on DJ30 companies, no trading cost

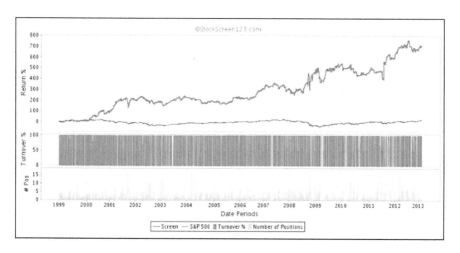

It looks nice, doesn't it ?

Now with trading costs = 0.1%:

Chart 7.2: simulation of the "4-2" strategy on DJ30 companies, 0.1% cost

Unfortunately in realistic conditions the return of this "profitable" strategy falls from 16% a year to negative.

Short selling

The only market where buying and selling are symmetric actions is forex. Buying a currency is selling another one. But short selling a stock or an ETF is not a similar operation to buying it.

First, you have to borrow it. The rate depends on your broker, and can change over time. The continued availability of the borrowed stocks and ETFs is not guaranteed for the retail investor. Your broker has the right to ask you – at any time – to buy them back. If you cannot do it yourself, the order is automatically forced. The only guarantee you have is that the price you get is between the low and the high of the current day.

When you buy a stock, your possible profit is potentially unlimited and your possible loss is limited to your initial position value plus trading fees. When selling short, your profit is limited to your initial position size minus borrowing and trading fees, your loss is potentially unlimited.

Short selling penny stocks is an especially risky sport. Selling short big caps is safer but can still lead to disaster.

In 2008, Volkswagen AG., was put in a "corner" by a major shareholder on the German stock market. The following short-squeeze was epic. The stock price skyrocketed from about 200 Euros to almost 1000 Euros in two days. Volkswagen became briefly the world's most valuable company before falling to its previous level. In the interval, short sellers covered their positions at any price, voluntarily or forced by their brokers. At least one of them committed suicide: a 75 year-old German billionaire and stock market veteran. Commodities are not exempt from the corner risk, with the example of silver in 1980.

The second reason to beware of short-selling strategies is that they cannot be simulated in a reliable way, because the required data don't exist. To my knowledge there is no database available to retail traders that can tell you that a stock "S" was shortable by a broker "B" from a date "D1" to a date "D2", with an average borrowing rate "R".

For ETFs, things are simpler in certain cases: more and more inverse ETFs allow investors to short-sell in a purchase, reducing the risk and making simulations possible. As these are still relatively recent instruments, the simulation interval is limited.

Complexity

Warren Buffett has written that we should invest only in something we can understand. If that is true for individual stocks, that is even more true for strategies.

You will be more confident by keeping things as simple as possible. It is also very often a clue of robustness.

Avoid proprietary features of your screener, simulation platform or software. You are the master of your investment only if your strategy is portable to another platform. Better, if once designed you can execute it without the help of a platform or software. Being an independent investor means keeping strategies as independent as possible of the tools.

In fundamental analysis, beware of indicators that may be different from one data provider to another. If you cannot perform simulations with various data sources, limit yourself to well-known indicators and make a sample test comparing data from different sources.

When working on a strategy, just as when working on software architectures or marketing systems, I have always kept in mind this quote of Antoine de Saint-Exupéry:

> *Perfection is achieved, not when there is nothing more to add, but when there is nothing left to take away.*

Another one, by Albert Einstein:

> *Make everything as simple as possible, but not simpler.*

Over-fitting

A risk when finding a good strategy is to think it better than it is in reality. The rules, parameter values, simulation interval, starting date, number of positions may be involuntarily optimized for a particular market situation, a particular set of instruments. If you make a backtest of holding all precious metals between 1999 and April 2011, you will have great results. Of course, the real mistakes are more difficult to detect.

The first and most efficient tool against over-fitting is common sense.

A reasonable simulation should:

- Have a sufficient number of decision points (let's say 100 or more).
- Contain at least a bull period, a bear period and a sideways period in the study interval.
- Show a significant outperformance with a broad enough range number of holdings (let's say, 4 to 15 positions).
- Give stable results with different starting dates (especially for monthly and quarterly rebalanced strategies).

A more formal way to detect over-fitting is to look for discontinuities. Consider your simulation as a mathematical function with multiple variables.

Think of every factor that may change the return: not only the parameters of your screener rules, but also the number of selected stocks/ETFs, rebalancing period, position size, starting date, slippage rate, etc.

Move all parameters one by one, looking at the influence on the return, drawdown, and maybe other indicators (Sortino ratio, Kelly criterion, drawdown durations for example).

Beware of sharp changes: discontinuities relative to variables are a sign of instability. Prefer an average and stable strategy than one with outstanding results on a very small variable range or with uncertain variables (slippage rate for small caps for example).

Last thing related to over-fitting: it is not advisable to begin investing in a strategy when the simulation shows that it is currently in its longest historical drawdown.

Misinterpretation

A simulation just gives you a data series. These data are useless, and may lead to a bad decision, if not correctly interpreted.

There are two risks:

- investing in a bad strategy (statisticians call it the alpha-risk), and
- rejecting a good one (the beta-risk).

The alpha-risk is the most harmful. With good money management it means the loss of all or a part of the allocated capital, and with a bad or non-existent money management it may be the way to financial ruin.

The beta-risk means just a missed opportunity. Missing an opportunity is not harmful. Except if it is a life-changing one. Or worse, if your decision process makes you miss opportunities systematically.

Your decision criteria should be tuned to reject all bad strategies, and accept a sufficient number of good ones. That's the theory. Practically, you will probably select your three or four best strategies based on different rules. It should be a minimum for an all-weather portfolio.

A common mistake is to focus on the return, whereas the most important factor is the drawdown, both from a psychological and financial point of view. Psychologically, because it is said that the pain to lose an amount of money is twice as intense as the pleasure to gain the same amount. Financially, because a low drawdown strategy might be leveraged and give better results than another one which has a higher return, but a volatility excluding leveraging.

You may want to fix limits for the historical maximum drawdowns and durations. The limits depend of course on the expected return and may be different from one investor to another. On weekly and monthly rebalancing, I consider acceptable strategies with historical individual drawdowns up to 35%, provided that their combination keep the global drawdowns well below the average return. You may also want to use the Sortino ratio and Kelly criterion to influence your opinion about a strategy.

Forgetting control

Track and compare real and simulated results when you are executing a strategy.

Investigate if you detect a divergence and don't hesitate to put a strategy in quarantine if you cannot find an acceptable explanation.

Using leveraged ETFs

Another – maybe less dangerous – mistake is to base a strategy on leveraged ETFs. These instruments have the objective to multiply performance, generally by a factor of 2 or 3.

First, some leveraged ETFs are not reliable for this objective. I have already seen a 2x long and a 2x short ETF on the same underlying asset going more than 1% in the same direction on the same daily close.

More disturbing, leveraging a daily performance has an inconvenient effect on a longer timescale. This is called beta-slippage.

To understand it, imagine a very volatile asset that goes up 25% on day 1 and down 20% on day 2.

A perfect double leveraged ETF goes up 50% on day 1 and down 40% on day 2.

On the close of day 2, the underlying asset is back to its initial price:

(1 + 0.25) x (1 - 0.2) = 1

And the perfect leveraged ETF?

(1 + 0.5) x (1 - 0.4) = 0.9

This is the magic of beta-slippage. Nothing has changed for the underlying asset, and yet 10% of your money has disappeared from the table.

Beta-slippage is not a scam: it is just the normal behavior of a leveraged daily-rebalanced portfolio. If you manage yourself a leveraged portfolio, you create your own beta-slippage at each rebalancing. The more frequent the rebalancing, the higher the risk that the result will diverge from your expectations.

The previous example is simple, but beta-slippage is not a simple mathematical object. It cannot be calculated from statistical and probabilistic parameters (even including the volatility). It depends on a specific sequence of gains and losses. So even in the perfect case, this makes questionable any backtest using a leveraged ETF. The results are much more dependent on a specific behavior than with other kinds of financial instruments. They are less representative of a statistical or probabilistic behavior that can be generalized for the future. It doesn't mean that a strategy on leveraged ETFs cannot work. Just that it needs more luck.

We have seen a theoretical and perfect example. In reality leveraged ETFs are impacted by other factors:

- **management fees,**
- **embedded options,** making the Net Asset Value (NAV) dependent of volatility,
- **embedded futures,** making the NAV dependent of rolling costs or gains,
- **skills and goodwill,** the manager can do anything that is not prohibited by the law and the product prospectus.

Leveraged ETFs are not bad products, in fact there are a few good ones that can be held with mid-term objectives. Nevertheless it is more reasonable to use them in a framework for which they have been designed: day-trading.

CHAPTER SUMMARY

- Some guidelines are given to investors to develop their own strategies.

- The first two choices to make are the trading style and the market anomaly, then come the tools.

- Some sources of mistakes are listed and explained: time, liquidity, costs, short-selling, complexity, over-fitting, misinterpretation, control, leveraged ETFs.

CONCLUSION

IS INVESTMENT A SCIENCE OR AN ART?

CERTAINLY BOTH, AND EACH INVESTOR has to find his or her own balance of the two. Although intuition and inspiration are key for many successful investors, most of them rely on indicators, calculations, methods and systems. Using indicators and modelization *should* be based on the *hope* to get a reproducible result with a probability and a confidence interval. The two most important words of this sentence are "should" and "hope".

"Should" because many traders and investors don't know the statistics and probabilities associated with the indicators and models they are using. Who knows the real probabilities behind a double top pattern, or a doji candlestick? They may be worse than you think.

"Hope" because there is no guarantee that a model will be valid forever. Its validity may depend on hypotheses we are unaware of, or that are undecidable. We live in a world of correlation, not of causality. A model is just a way to link inputs to outputs with probabilities, not to explain them in a "cause-consequence" paradigm. Geniuses like Galileo, Newton, Einstein, Planck, and others have progressively changed our scientific vision of the world from a flat Earth to a probabilist view of mechanics. If even mechanics relies on probabilities now, what do you think is a cause or consequence in economics and finance? By the way are we sure that we are speaking of economics and finance? Modeling investment strategies is more about modeling the expected reaction of a group ("the market") to a measured stimulus. As a subject of research, it might be closer to experimental psychology, a field opened in the 19th century by German scientists.

We are now at the end of this book. If you find that there's nothing new here, you are right. What has a better probability to work in the future is what has been working for years, decades and sometimes centuries. The financial markets are the result of human behaviors. The new financial products, the availability of real-time data, the internet, high frequency trading... are merely amplifiers and accelerators. Underlying human nature has not changed for centuries and longer. As investors we must beware of the it-is-all-different-now myth. The combination of stimuli is always different. The reactions are always based on the same rules, now amplified and accelerated by informational and financial engineering.

That men do not learn very much from the lessons of history is the most important of all the lessons that history has to teach.

This sentence of Aldous Huxley probably explains why human beings have a tendency to reproduce the same behavioral patterns. An investor's job should be to identify a set of robust behavioral patterns in the financial markets, then bet a reasonable amount on them.

I hope you have found in this book some new ideas for researching, classifying, interpreting and implementing old patterns.

APPENDICES

APPENDIX 1:
SUMMER AND WINTER RETURNS SINCE 1950

THE FOLLOWING TABLE GIVES the Dow Jones Industrial Average return season by season from 1950 to 2011 (source of yearly seasonal returns: *Market Seasonality: Capitalizing Upon Summer Decline* by M. Blumer on Seeking Alpha website, source of total returns and drawdowns: my own calculation).

These statistics are from May to May. It means that the line N counts returns from May 1st of year N to Apr 30th of year N+1. It also means that compounding the returns of summer and winter on line N doesn't give the return of year N.

DJIA	% May-Oct	Total Return	Drawdown	% Nov-Apr	Total Return	Drawdown
1950	5.0	5.0	0.0	15.2	15.2	0.0
1951	1.2	6.3	0.0	-1.8	13.1	-1.8
1952	4.5	11.0	0.0	2.1	15.5	0.0
1953	0.4	11.5	0.0	15.8	33.8	0.0
1954	10.3	23.0	0.0	20.9	61.7	0.0
1955	6.9	31.5	0.0	13.5	83.5	0.0
1956	-7.0	22.3	-7.0	3.0	89.0	0.0
1957	-10.8	9.0	-17.0	3.4	95.5	0.0
1958	19.2	30.0	-1.1	14.8	124.4	0.0

DJIA	% May-Oct	Total Return	Drawdown	% Nov-Apr	Total Return	Drawdown
1959	3.7	34.8	0.0	-6.9	108.9	-6.9
1960	-3.5	30.1	-3.5	16.9	144.2	0.0
1961	3.7	34.9	0.0	-5.5	130.8	-5.5
1962	-11.4	19.5	-11.4	21.7	180.9	0.0
1963	5.2	25.7	-6.8	7.4	201.7	0.0
1964	7.7	35.4	0.0	5.6	218.5	0.0
1965	4.2	41.1	0.0	-2.8	209.6	-2.8
1966	-13.6	21.9	-13.6	11.1	244.0	0.0
1967	-1.9	19.6	-15.2	3.7	256.7	0.0
1968	4.4	24.9	-11.5	-0.2	256.0	-0.2
1969	-9.9	12.5	-20.3	-14.0	206.2	-14.2
1970	2.7	15.5	-18.1	24.6	281.5	0.0
1971	-10.9	2.9	-27.0	13.7	333.8	0.0
1972	0.1	3.0	-27.0	-3.6	318.1	-3.6
1973	3.8	7.0	-24.2	-12.5	265.9	-15.7
1974	-20.5	-15.0	-39.7	23.4	351.5	0.0
1975	1.8	-13.4	-38.7	19.2	438.2	0.0
1976	-3.2	-16.2	-40.6	-3.9	417.2	-3.9
1977	-11.7	-26.0	-47.6	2.3	429.1	-1.7
1978	-5.4	-30.0	-50.4	7.9	470.9	0.0
1979	-4.6	-33.2	-52.7	0.2	472.0	0.0
1980	13.1	-24.5	-46.5	7.9	517.2	0.0
1981	-14.6	-35.5	-54.3	-0.5	514.1	-0.5
1982	16.9	-24.6	-46.6	23.6	659.0	0.0
1983	-0.1	-24.7	-46.6	-4.4	625.6	-4.4
1984	3.1	-22.3	-45.0	4.2	656.1	-0.4
1985	9.2	-15.2	-39.9	29.8	881.5	0.0

DJIA	% May-Oct	Total Return	Drawdown	% Nov-Apr	Total Return	Drawdown
1986	5.3	-10.7	-36.7	21.8	1095.4	0.0
1987	-12.8	-22.1	-44.8	1.9	1118.1	0.0
1988	5.7	-17.7	-41.7	12.6	1271.6	0.0
1989	9.4	-10.0	-36.2	0.4	1277.1	0.0
1990	-8.1	-17.3	-41.4	18.2	1527.7	0.0
1991	6.3	-12.0	-37.7	9.4	1680.7	0.0
1992	-4.0	-15.6	-40.2	6.2	1791.1	0.0
1993	7.4	-9.3	-35.7	0.0	1791.7	0.0
1994	6.2	-3.7	-31.7	10.6	1992.2	0.0
1995	10.0	5.9	-24.9	17.1	2350.0	0.0
1996	8.3	14.7	-18.7	16.2	2746.9	0.0
1997	6.2	21.8	-13.6	21.8	3367.5	0.0
1998	-5.2	15.5	-18.1	25.6	4255.2	0.0
1999	-0.5	14.9	-18.5	0.0	4256.9	0.0
2000	2.2	17.5	-16.8	-2.2	4161.1	-2.2
2001	-15.5	-0.7	-29.7	9.6	4570.1	0.0
2002	-15.6	-16.2	-40.6	1.0	4616.9	0.0
2003	15.6	-3.2	-31.4	4.3	4819.7	0.0
2004	-1.9	-5.0	-32.7	1.7	4903.3	0.0
2005	2.4	-2.7	-31.1	8.9	5348.6	0.0
2006	6.3	3.4	-26.7	8.1	5789.9	0.0
2007	6.6	10.2	-21.9	-8.0	5318.7	-8.0
2008	-27.3	-19.9	-43.2	-12.4	4646.8	-19.4
2009	18.9	-4.7	-32.5	13.3	5278.1	-8.7
2010	1.0	-3.8	-31.8	15.2	6095.6	0.0
2011	-6.7	-10.2	-36.4	13.3	6919.6	0.0

APPENDIX 2:
A NEW KIND OF QUANTITATIVE INDICATOR

This is an introduction to behavioral indicators that have been used for years in marketing. It shows that the peaks of requests for specific keywords in the Google search engine has been associated with most corrections in the Apple share price [AAPL] since 2006. The signal was particularly accurate in September 2012.

Note: No analysis or opinion of AAPL is provided here.

When everyone is talking about a stock, it's often time to sell. If you know how to use it, Google Trends tells you what everyone is thinking and talking about.

Below are the Google Trends search volume charts for the keywords *AAPL price*, *apple stock price* and *apple share price* since 2004. They represent the number of requests from people who want information about the price of AAPL.

Chart A2.1: Google search volume about AAPL

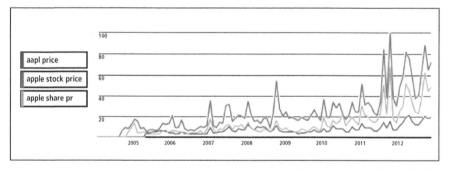

Google Trends also allows you to track the geographical distribution of the requests: *AAPL price* is more used in North America, *apple share price* in the UK, Oceania and Southern Asia, *apple stock price* all over the world.

Chart A2.2: relative search volume by keyword and country

Chart courtesy of Google Inc

The three request categories are strongly correlated. As *apple stock price* is the most used worldwide, my indicator is based on it.

I consider that there is a signal when **the search volume has a new high at twice the "current noise level" or more**. I call "current noise level" the average search volume of the previous months.

This is the search volume chart for 2012:

Chart A2.3: 2012 search volume for 'apple stock price' courtesy of Google Inc

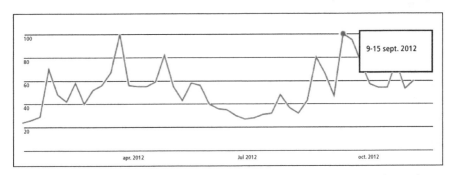

Chart courtesy of Google Inc.

Two strong signals were given in March and September 2012. Exploring the search volume chart on a weekly timescale, nine signals have been given by Google Trends on "apple stock price" since 2004. I have listed them and checked if they were accurate (correlated with a mid-term leg down), inaccurate (correlated with a mid-term leg up), or neutral (no significant trend next three months or more). When it was accurate, I have verified if the signal was usable. It means checking that AAPL was still high enough the 1st day after the weekly signal to sell and avoid the leg down.

The nine signals are listed in the following table.

1	**January 2005** (week 9th to 15th)	Inaccurate (rally following)
2	**January 2006** (week 8th to 14th)	Accurate and usable. The 1st day after the signal (17th of January) was almost the top before a long and deep drawdown.
3	**January 2007** (week 7th to 13rd)	Accurate and usable. The day after the signal (strangely, the 17th of January again) was close to a top before a quick drop. There was also a double-top pattern on the price. The Google Trends signal was sent before its validation.
4	**October 2008** (week 5th to 11th)	Neutral
5	**January 2011** (week 16th to 22nd)	Neutral
6	**August 2011** (weeks 7th to 13rd and 21st to 27th)	Neutral
7	**October 2011** (week 2nd to 8th)	Neutral
8	**March 2012** (week 18th to 24th)	Accurate and usable. The day after the signal (the 27th of March) was close to a top before a significant drawdown. There was also a head-and-shoulders chart pattern. The Google Trends signal was sent before. The current price (at the time this book is written) is well below this level again.
9	**September 2012** (week 9th to 15th)	Very accurate and usable. The first open day after the signal week was the 17th of September. Selling on the 17th would have avoided the 2012-2013 big correction, and also allowed you to go out right at the top.

Only two major corrections since 2004 have not been preceded by a Google Trends signal, in January 2008 and August-October 2008. The first one was specific to AAPL, the second one was the global market crash.

To summarize, Google Trends has given nine sell signals on AAPL since 2004. It was accurate and usable four times, neutral four times and inaccurate once. When accurate it always signaled close to a top, and once almost right at one (17th September 2012). It has missed only one big correction specific to the stock.

You may wonder if an indicator that is right 4 times out of 9 is worth a look?

My opinion is that "neutral" is accurate: if there is a 8/9 probability for a stock to go down *or nowhere* in the following months, I think that money is better elsewhere. Of course, selling out is a risk to miss the next rally. Google Trends signals don't signal when to buy again. But technical signals on price and volume can do that.

You may also think that the data sample is too small?

A 8/9 ratio means a calculated probability of 57% with a 95% confidence interval. In other words, there is a 95% chance that the real success rate is *higher* than 57%. This is better than most popular signals used every day by investors.

According to my observations, not only on AAPL but also on other assets, Relative Search Volume (RSV) peaks in Google Trends may be useful at least as warnings, and sometimes as sell signals. More research is needed to figure out if it is possible to identify a more precise definition for the noise level and the RSV indicator, and generalize it across assets.

Google Trends is worth a look for fashionable and controversial investments that generate a lot of Google requests. But it is difficult or impossible to use for most stocks and assets because of low search volumes and weak signals.

APPENDIX 3:
BIBLIOGRAPHY AND SOURCES

BILBLIOGRAPHY

ETF Trading Strategies Revealed, David Vomund, 2006

Are Monthly Seasonals Real? A Three Century Perspective, B. Jacobsen and C. Y. Zhang, SSRN 2012

The Halloween Indicator: Everywhere and all the time, B. Jacobsen and C. Y. Zhang, SSRN 2012

The Optimism Cycle: Sell in May, R. Q. Doeswijk, 2005

Paired-switching for tactical portfolio allocation, A.Maewal and J.Bock, SSRN 2011

A Quantitative Approach to Tactical Asset Allocation, M.T. Faber, *Journal of Wealth Management*, 2007

Relative Strength Strategies for Investing, M.T. Faber, Cambria Investment Management, 2010

Where the Black Swans Hide & the 10 Best Days Myth, M.T. Faber, Cambria Investment Management, 2011

Risk Premia Harvesting Through Dual Momentum, Gary Antonacci, 2012

Momentum Strategies in Futures Markets and Trend-Following Funds, Nick Baltas and Robert Kosowski, 2013

ONLINE SOURCES

www.ssrn.com
www.seasonalcharts.com
www.seekingalpha.com

APPENDIX 4:
SUPPORT

All the strategies described in this book can be implemented and executed without any additional product or service.

At the time this book is published, a free subscription-based service is available at:

http://stratecode.com

The free service includes:

- An extended free trial offer of Portfolio123

- The code and parameters of some strategies described in the book

- Possible updates and corrections to this book

- An e-mail address to contact me: **stratecode@gmail.com** (my ability to answer depends on the number of messages and current workload).

The website, service and Portfolio123 extended free trial offer may be modified, closed to new subscribers or terminated for any reason without previous notice.

INDEX

CPSIA information can be obtained at www.ICGtesting.com
Printed in the USA
LVOW01s1843261014

410572LV00002BA/6/P

9 780857 193001